MCAT®

Critical Analysis and Reasoning Skills Review

Edited by Alexander Stone Macnow, MD

KAPLAN

PUBLISHING

New York

© 2014 by Kaplan, Inc.

Published by Kaplan Publishing, a division of Kaplan, Inc.
395 Hudson Street
New York, NY 10014

Printed in the United States of America

10 9 8 7 6 5 4 3 2

ISBN: 978-1-61865-608-7

Kaplan Publishing books are available at special quantity discounts to use for sales promotions, employee premiums, or educational purposes. For more information or to purchase books, please call the Simon & Schuster special sales department at 866-506-1949.

The *Kaplan MCAT Review* Team

Alexander Stone Macnow, MD

Editor-in-Chief

M. Dominic Eggert

Kaplan MCAT Faculty

Kimberly Sinnott, MA

Kaplan MCAT Faculty

MCAT faculty reviewers Elmar R. Aliyev; James Burns; Jonathan Cornfield; Alisha Maureen Crowley; Nikolai Dorofeev, MD; Benjamin Downer, MS; Colin Doyle; Marilyn Engle; Eleni M. Eren; Raef Ali Fadel; Tyra Hall-Pogar, PhD; Scott Huff; Samer T. Ismail; Elizabeth A. Kudlaty; Kelly Kyker-Snowman, MS; Ningfei Li; John P. Mahon; Matthew A. Meier; Nainika Nanda; Caroline Nkemdilim Opene; Kaitlyn E. Prenger; Uneeb Qureshi; Derek Rusnak, MA; Kristen L. Russell, ME; Bela G. Starkman, PhD; Michael Paul Tomani, MS; Nicholas M. White; Kerranna Williamson, MBA; Allison Ann Wilkes, MS; and Tony Yu

Thanks to Kim Bowers; Tim Eich; Samantha Fallon; Owen Farcy; Dan Frey; Robin Garmise; Rita Garthaffner; Joanna Graham; Adam Grey; Allison Harm; Beth Hoffberg; Aaron Lemon-Strauss; Keith Lubeley; Diane McGarvey; Petros Minasi; John Polstein; Deeangelee Pooran-Kublall, MD, MPH; Rochelle Rothstein, MD; Larry Rudman; Sylvia Tidwell Scheuring; Carly Schnur; Karin Tucker; Lee Weiss; and the countless others who made this project possible.

About the MCAT

The structure of the four sections of the MCAT is shown below.

Chemical and Physical Foundations of Biological Systems	
Time	95 minutes
Format	• 59 questions • Score between 118 and 132 • Most questions are passage-based, but some are discrete (stand-alone) questions
What It Tests	• Biochemistry: 25% • Biology: 5% • General Chemistry: 30% • Organic Chemistry: 15% • Physics: 25%

Critical Analysis and Reasoning Skills (CARS)	
Time	90 minutes
Format	• 53 questions • Score between 118 and 132 • All questions are passage-based. There are no discrete (stand-alone) questions.
What It Tests	Disciplines: • Humanities: 50% • Social Sciences: 50% Skills: • *Foundations of Comprehension*: 30% • *Reasoning Within the Text*: 30% • *Reasoning Beyond the Text*: 40%

Biological and Biochemical Foundations of Living Systems	
Time	95 minutes
Format	• 59 questions • Score between 118 and 132 • Most questions are passage-based, but some are discrete (stand-alone) questions
What It Tests	• Biochemistry: 25% • Biology: 65% • General Chemistry: 5% • Organic Chemistry: 5%

KAPLAN

Psychological, Social, and Biological Foundations of Behavior	
Time	95 minutes
Format	• 59 questions • Score between 118 and 132 • Most questions are passage-based, but some are discrete (stand-alone) questions
What It Tests	• Biology: 5% • Psychology: 65% • Sociology: 30%
Total	
Testing Time	375 minutes (6 hours, 15 minutes)
Questions	230
Score	472 to 528

The MCAT also tests four *Scientific Inquiry and Reasoning Skills* (SIRS):

1. Knowledge of Scientific Concepts and Principles (35% of questions)
2. Scientific Reasoning and Problem-Solving (45% of questions)
3. Reasoning About the Design and Execution of Research (10% of questions)
4. Data-Based and Statistical Reasoning (10% of questions)

The MCAT is a computer-based test (CBT) and is offered at Prometric centers during almost every month of the year. There are optional breaks between each section, and there is a lunch break between the second and third section of the exam.

Register online for the MCAT at www.aamc.org/mcat.

For further questions, contact the MCAT team at the Association of American Medical Colleges:

MCAT Resource Center
Association of American Medical Colleges

(202) 828-0690
www.aamc.org/mcat
mcat@aamc.org

How This Book Was Created

The *Kaplan MCAT Review* project began in November 2012 shortly after the release of the *Preview Guide for the MCAT 2015 Exam*, 2nd edition. Through thorough analysis by our staff psychometricians, we were able to analyze the relative yield of the different topics on the MCAT, and we began constructing tables of contents for the books of the *Kaplan MCAT Review* series.

Writing of the books began in April 2013. A dedicated staff of 19 writers, 7 editors, and 32 proofreaders worked over 5000 combined hours to produce these books. The format of the books was heavily influenced by weekly meetings with Kaplan's learning-science team.

These books were submitted for publication in late March and early April 2014. For any updates after this date, please visit www.kaplanmcat.com.

The information presented in these books covers everything listed on the official MCAT content lists—nothing more, nothing less. Every topic in these lists is covered in the same level of detail as is common to the undergraduate and postbaccalaureate classes that are considered prerequisites for the MCAT. Note that your premedical classes may cover topics not discussed in these books, or they may go into more depth than these books do. Additional exposure to science content is never a bad thing, but recognize that all of the content knowledge you are expected to have walking in on Test Day is covered in these books.

If you have any questions about the content presented here, email KaplanMCATfeedback@kaplan.com. For other questions not related to content, email booksupport@kaplan.com.

Each book has been vetted through at least six rounds of review. To that end, the information presented is these books is true and accurate to the best of our knowledge. Still, your feedback helps us improve our prep materials. Please notify us of any inaccuracies or errors in the books by sending an email to KaplanMCATfeedback@kaplan.com.

Using This Book

Kaplan MCAT Critical Analysis and Reasoning Skills Review, along with the other six books in the *Kaplan MCAT Review* series, brings the Kaplan classroom experience to you—right in your home, at your convenience. This book offers the same Kaplan content review, strategies, and practice that make Kaplan the #1 choice for MCAT prep. After all, twice as many doctors prepared with Kaplan for the MCAT than with any other course.

This book is designed to help you review the *Critical Analysis and Reasoning Skills* section of the MCAT. It represents one of the content review resources available to you. Additional review is available in your Online Center, including more practice questions and full-length practice exams. Register for your Online Center at kaptest.com/booksonline.

Unlike the other books in this MCAT series, there is no content to review for the *Critical Analysis and Reasoning Skills* section. The questions are written in such a way that they do not presume any prior fund of knowledge. In other words, all the support that is needed to answer the questions correctly is found in the corresponding passages.

SIDEBARS

The following is a guide to the five types of sidebars you'll find in *Kaplan MCAT Critical Analysis and Reasoning Skills Review*:

- **Bridge**: These sidebars create connections between science topics that appear in multiple chapters throughout the *Kaplan MCAT Review* series.
- **Key Concept**: These sidebars draw attention to the most important takeaways in a given topic, and they sometimes offer synopses or overviews of complex information. If you understand nothing else, make sure you grasp the Key Concepts for any given subject.
- **MCAT Expertise**: These sidebars point out how information may be tested on the MCAT or offer key strategy points and test-taking tips that you should apply on Test Day.
- **Real World**: These sidebars illustrate how a concept in the text relates to the practice of medicine or the world at large. While this is not information you need to know for Test Day, many of the topics in Real World sidebars are excellent examples of how a concept may appear in a passage or question on the MCAT.

In this end, this is your book, so write in the margins, draw diagrams, highlight the key points—do whatever is necessary to help you get that higher score. We look forward to working with you as you achieve your dreams and become the doctor you deserve to be!

Contents

About CARS

In This Chapter

Introduction

Congratulations! You are about to embark upon an exciting journey down the path to medical school to achieve your goal of becoming a doctor. Like any major journey in life, this will require thorough preparation. Fortunately, you don't have to prepare for this journey on your own: Kaplan offers comprehensive preparation for the MCAT with proven strategies that can enhance your score in all sections of the exam.

As a premedical student, you have already been exposed to a wide variety of science topics, which will be tested in the three science sections of the test. In contrast, the *Critical Analysis and Reasoning Skills* (CARS) section will present you with an array of passages from various disciplines to which you may have never been exposed—for example, a musicological analysis of Johannes Brahms's 1868 masterpiece *Ein Deutsches Requiem*, a philosophical diatribe criticizing Immanuel Kant's *Metaphysics*, or a dissection of the political underpinnings of the development of the Medicare system—and you will be expected to read, understand, and apply this knowledge. Students often find themselves overwhelmed or feel ill-equipped for the CARS section of the test, but Kaplan is here to help! This book will help you understand what is expected of you in CARS and presents the Kaplan strategies that have paved the way for many thousands of students to become the doctors they deserve to be.

In this chapter, we will go over the structure of the CARS section of the MCAT, as well as the diverse disciplines encountered in CARS passages. We'll provide a brief overview of the question categories identified by the Association of American Medical Colleges (AAMC). Finally, we'll discuss how to use this book and how it can guide you in preparing for your MCAT and the journey beyond. The journey to becoming a physician may be long, but it is ultimately extremely rewarding. Some day in the future, you'll find yourself donning your white coat, changing patients' lives, and realizing that having the right plan for success is what made the journey possible.

1.1 The CARS Section

In some ways, the *Critical Analysis and Reasoning Skills* (CARS) section of the MCAT will be nothing new to you; it is similar to many of the standardized tests you have taken throughout your academic career, presenting you with passages to read and multiple choice questions to gauge your understanding. In 90 minutes, you will be presented with passages, each of which will be followed by approximately 5 to 7 questions, for a total of 53 questions. The passages you encounter will be relatively short (but lengthier than the science passages on the test), ranging from 500 to 600 words.

Unlike reading comprehension sections you have come across previously, such as those in the SAT® or ACT®, the CARS section of the MCAT has been designed to assess analytical and reasoning skills that are required in medical school. The passages you will face in CARS will be multifaceted, incorporating advanced vocabulary, presenting varied writing styles, and requiring higher-level thought. To answer the accompanying questions, you will have to go beyond merely comprehending the content of a CARS passage: you will need to analyze its rhetorical and logical structure, and even be able to assess how it impacts (or is impacted by) outside information.

1.2 Passages

The types of passages chosen for CARS consist of multiple paragraphs that require active, critical reading to answer the questions that follow. The passages included on the section are from an array of disciplines in the social sciences and humanities, as listed in Table 1.1. Approximately half of the passages (and questions) that you encounter on Test Day will fall in the realm of the humanities, while the other half will be in the social sciences. All of the passages that appear in CARS are selected from books, journals, and other publications similar to those you have come across in academic settings.

Humanities	Social Sciences
Architecture	Anthropology
Art	Archaeology
Dance	Economics
Ethics	Education
Literature	Geography
Music	History
Philosophy	Linguistics
Popular Culture	Political Science
Religion	Population Health
Studies of Diverse Cultures*	Psychology
Theater	Sociology
	Studies of Diverse Cultures*

* Note: Studies of Diverse Cultures can be tested in both humanities and social sciences passages.

Table 1.1. Humanities and Social Sciences Disciplines in the CARS Section[1]

For students who have exclusively focused on the sciences, information for the fields used in the CARS section may be presented in a strikingly different way that can sometimes seem overwhelming. This book will review the writing styles used for the passages in CARS and explain how to read these passages with purpose, which will ultimately make them much less intimidating and significantly more manageable.

1.3 Question Categories

The AAMC has identified three categories of questions in CARS that will assess your critical thinking skills: *Foundations of Comprehension*, *Reasoning Within the Text*, and *Reasoning Beyond the Text* questions.

FOUNDATIONS OF COMPREHENSION

These questions tend to be straightforward. They will ask about the main ideas of a passage, specific details from within the passage, the purpose of a given part of the passage, or the likely meaning of a word or phrase based on context. These questions are the most similar to those you have seen in previous standardized tests because they only ask for reading comprehension (understanding what you have read). Questions in *Foundations of Comprehension* will make up 30 percent of the questions in CARS.

1. From *The Official Guide to the MCAT 2015 Exam*, 4th Edition.

In Chapter 9 of *MCAT CARS Review*, we will further dissect the four question types within *Foundations of Comprehension*:

- Main Idea
- Detail
- Function
- Definition-in-Context

REASONING WITHIN THE TEXT

Reasoning Within the Text questions require greater thought than *Foundations of Comprehension* questions because they will ask you to draw inferences (unstated parts of arguments that logically must be true based on the information given) or ask how one piece of information relates to another (as a piece of evidence that supports a conclusion, for example). Questions in *Reasoning Within the Text* will make up 30 percent of the questions in CARS.

In Chapter 10 of *MCAT CARS Review*, we will further dissect the two main question types within *Reasoning Within the Text* and a few other, rare questions that fit into this category:

- Inference
- Strengthen–Weaken (Within the Passage)

REASONING BEYOND THE TEXT

Reasoning Beyond the Text questions focus on two specific skills: first, the capacity to extrapolate information from the passage and place it within new contexts and, second, the ability to ascertain how new information would relate to and affect the concepts in the passage. Questions in *Reasoning Beyond the Text* will make up 40 percent of the questions in CARS.

In Chapter 11 of *MCAT CARS Review*, we will further dissect the two main question types within *Reasoning Beyond the Text* and a few other, rare questions that fit into this category:

- Apply
- Strengthen–Weaken (Beyond the Passage)

Conclusion

This chapter is only a beginning. Now that we have covered the structure of the CARS section, we will dive into the Kaplan strategies that will help you score points on Test Day. In Chapter 2, we will begin with an analysis of rhetoric, exploring how a passage's author creates a conduit for the transmission of a message to an audience.

In Chapter 3, we will discuss critical reading and, specifically, how keywords will underlie your ability to master all four modes of reading. We continue that conversation in Chapter 4 through the Kaplan Method for CARS Passages. Chapters 5 and 6 similarly constitute a single unit; in Chapter 5, we look at how arguments are constructed, and in Chapter 6, we bring in introductory formal logic to create a systematized approach to these arguments. Chapter 7 serves as a turning point as we segue from discussing the varieties of passages and common passage structures to anticipating questions. In Chapter 8, we introduce the Kaplan Method for CARS Questions, and then we see its application, in the three following chapters, in each of the different AAMC categories. Finally, we end with a look at how to review your practice tests to find your personal test-taking pathologies and keep improving that score.

CONCEPT AND STRATEGY SUMMARY

The CARS Section

- The *Critical Analysis and Reasoning Skills* (CARS) section lasts 90 minutes and contains 53 questions.

  ○ Passages range from 500 to 600 words.

  ○ Each passage has approximately 5 to 7 questions.

- CARS requires going beyond merely comprehending the content: you must analyze a passage's rhetorical and logical structure, and even be able to assess relationships with new outside information.

Passages

- Half of the passages will be in the humanities (architecture, art, dance, ethics, literature, music, philosophy, popular culture, religion, studies of diverse cultures, and theater).

- Half of the passages will be in the social sciences (anthropology, archaeology, economics, education, geography, history, linguistics, political science, population health, psychology, sociology, and studies of diverse cultures).

Question Categories

- *Foundations of Comprehension* questions ask about the main ideas of a passage, specific details from within the passage, the purpose of a given part of the passage, or the likely meaning of a word or phrase based on context.

- *Reasoning Within the Text* questions ask you to draw inferences (unstated parts of arguments that logically must be true based on the information given) or ask how one piece of information relates to another (as a piece of evidence that supports a conclusion, for example).

- *Reasoning Beyond the Text* questions ask you to extrapolate information from the passage and place it within a new context or to ascertain how new information would relate to and affect the concepts in the passage.

Analyzing Rhetoric

In This Chapter

Introduction

You turn on the television and see a grainy, black-and-white, unflattering portrait of a woman with disconcerting statistics displayed to her right, ominous music in the background, and a narrator who sounds apprehensive as he recites all of her apparent flaws. *Another one of those stupid political attack ads*, you think as you flip the channel. Suddenly you find yourself confronted with startling images of malnourished children surrounded by filth as you hear a woman talking about *the importance of your donation*. You immediately recognize this as a commercial for a charitable organization and quietly change channels again to avoid feeling guilty. Now, an educated man standing behind a podium appears on the screen, droning on in a monotone about why his interpretation of the causes of the War of 1812 is the correct one. *Must be one of those public-access educational channels*, you conclude. *Maybe I should just get back to studying for my MCAT.* Though you may not realize it as you put down your remote control, simply by making conclusions about what you were watching on TV, you were engaged in rhetorical analysis.

In this chapter, we will take a more systematic approach to analyzing rhetoric. First, we will define the terms used in rhetoric and consider how rhetoric plays a role in daily life. Then, we will demonstrate the application of this knowledge to the MCAT. As you read, you will come to see the role rhetoric has already played in your life as a student and the value of increasing your awareness of it as you study for the CARS section. Why are rhetorical skills tested on the MCAT? Ultimately, a keen awareness of the topics discussed in this chapter will help you think critically about *how* information is delivered in medical school and beyond.

2.1 What Is Rhetoric?

Most of us are familiar with the device known as a rhetorical question. Although it ends in a question mark, a rhetorical question tends to have only one plausible and obvious answer. What makes it rhetorically effective is that it forces readers to reach the conclusion themselves, so they are more convinced of it than if the author had simply stated it. However, there are many more nuances to rhetoric than questions that aren't really questions. Considered broadly, **rhetoric** is the art of effective communication, both in speech and in text. Because the MCAT is a written exam, we will predominantly discuss the textual side of rhetoric throughout this chapter. While language may serve many purposes, the study of rhetoric tends to focus on persuasion—the attempt to influence others to adopt particular beliefs or engage in certain behaviors. **Rhetorical analysis**, then, is an examination of speech or writing that goes beyond *what* the author is saying (the content) to consider *how* the author is saying it, with a particular emphasis on techniques of persuasion.

When the *Writing Sample* was a section on the MCAT (from 1991 to 2013), effective *use* of rhetoric was an important skill to hone for Test Day. While premedical students still need to be able to write clearly for the Personal Statement and other application essays, your principal concern in the CARS section will be to understand how *other* people use rhetoric, in other words, to use rhetorical analysis. To that end, we will begin by defining several of the fundamental aspects of rhetoric: author, audience, message, goal, and context. To that end, we will then discuss some more subtle elements of rhetoric. Together, these constitute what we'll call **rhetorical knowledge**—an awareness of the other aspects of a text besides its content—which is necessary for the process of rhetorical analysis.

2.2 Key Components of Rhetoric

Key Concept

The rhetorical situation focuses on the transmission of ideas from the author to the audience, with a particular goal in mind.

The **rhetorical situation** is a way of representing any act of communication, emphasizing the transmission of ideas from an individual to an audience. Effective authors are rhetorically savvy and will direct their message to a particular subset of people with a clear goal in mind. Before placing pen to paper, or tapping out thoughts on the keyboard, the writer must answer the questions *To whom am I writing?* and *Why?*

AUTHOR

The **author**, in the most basic sense, is the individual or group writing the text. Authors can be distinguished by how much expertise they have on the topic at hand, by how passionate or vested in the topic they are, and by the groups or stakeholders they represent.

Authors who are expert in a topic—and who know that their intended audiences are also knowledgeable in the topic—tend to use a lot of jargon in their writing. **Jargon** refers to technical words and phrases that belong to a particular field. For example, *transcriptional repression*, *zwitterion*, and *anabolism* are all biochemical jargon words; *homunculus*, *Gesellschaften*, and *negative symptoms* are all behavioral sciences jargon words. Authors who are less expert, or who are writing to a less-informed audience, tend to use more common terminology and provide more explicitly detailed descriptions of their ideas. Authors who consider themselves less expert than their audiences may use an abundance of Moderating keywords, described in Chapter 3 of *MCAT CARS Review*.

When an author is passionate about the topic he is addressing, this emotion often manifests as strong language. Extreme keywords, also described in Chapter 3 of *MCAT CARS Review*, may suggest that an author is emotionally invested in the piece. Less-invested authors may use more emotionally neutral words to describe the same ideas.

Finally, an author may be writing on behalf of a larger group or body of stakeholders—individuals who also have an interest in the outcome of the written piece. This is sometimes indicated by an author's use of the word *we* rather than *I*. When speaking for others, authors may strengthen or weaken the representation of their opinions in the piece to match those of the rest of the group.

AUDIENCE

The **audience** is the person, or persons, for whom the text is intended. In daily life, the audience could be a single person with whom you have a dialogue, but publications typically have considerably larger audiences. Many CARS passages address an academic audience—perhaps other specialists in the author's field. Even when writing for the "general public," authors will draw upon idioms, clichés, symbols, and references that are recognizable only to people of a particular time and place. Because of the wide availability of many academic journals and historical documents, the author's message may reach a much wider audience than the author originally intended.

Regardless of whom the piece is written for, each person who reads it will approach the text differently. Nevertheless, readers who share many characteristics will tend to interpret the work in similar ways. For instance, students preparing to take the MCAT tend to share a science background that people who are interested in pursuing a business degree may lack. A business student might respond well to an article on the profitability of an industrial chemical process, but the same reader would likely need additional background to read a piece that proposed a theoretical mechanism explaining the reaction's kinetics. An MCAT student, on the other hand, may have more difficulty navigating complex business terminology but would certainly

MCAT Expertise

The more knowledgeable the author is on a topic, the more jargon he may use. This may make for a challenging passage to read, but recognize the MCAT does not expect you to know any field-specific terminology in CARS. Any important jargon words will be defined in the passage—or their definitions will be strongly implied.

be able to understand the mechanism description after reading Chapter 5 of *MCAT General Chemistry Review*. In CARS, you will rarely be a member of the intended audience, but you can still develop the ability to recognize for whom a passage was originally written.

MESSAGE

The **message** is the actual text that the author writes. This may be a physical document—as in the case of a journal article, book, or email—or it may be delivered verbally. It is important to note that the message itself contains only the explicit information offered by the author—the facts, data, and concepts the author draws upon, as well as any stated opinions.

The CARS section is unique in that many of its questions are not solely focused on the message the author has written but instead emphasize the goal and context of the piece. Whereas many other standardized tests focus predominantly on understanding what the author has said, the MCAT takes it a step further, sometimes asking you to use the text to glean characteristics about the author herself (including biases, assumptions, and even identity markers such as profession or nationality).

Voice

The author's **voice** is her unique style while writing. The author's word choice and the way she strings words together will differ from that of any other author, and may offer hints about her personality or other aspects of her identity. For example, you may be able to identify which of your friends wrote a particular email based solely on its wording. In CARS passages, quotations from other writers will present a different voice than that used by the author of the passage.

Genre and Medium

The **genre** is the category into which the written work can be placed. Genre encompasses a wide array of classifications, including fiction, nonfiction, drama, poetry, and so on. Genre can also represent the more concrete form of the work: a book, scholarly journal article, case study, essay, letter, email communication, and so forth. The audience and goal will necessarily affect what genre the author uses for the piece.

The **medium** is the delivery system into which the written work can be placed. In other words, it is the method used to transfer the message from the author to the audience. Examples of media include print (such as books, academic journals, newspapers, or pamphlets), broadcast (television, radio, music), and digital (email, text messages, social networking).

Bridge

An author's voice is related to two components of language theory: syntax (word choice and word order) and pragmatics (adapting one's message depending on the social context). Language theory is discussed in Chapter 4 of *MCAT Behavioral Sciences Review*.

Real World

Why do the testmakers care so much about your ability to think beyond just the message of an author's writing? This is a skill you'll use every day when talking with patients (to discern what a patient is really thinking from his body language and tone of voice) and when critically appraising research (to look for potential biases or conflicts of interest on the part of the researcher). To make good choices for your patients, you must be able to move beyond simply reading words on a page (message) and consider the bigger picture (goal and context).

GOAL

The **goal** is the author's intended outcome—the effect that she wishes to produce with her writing. In some cases, the author's goal may be simply to inform the audience. Passages with an informative goal tend to read like textbooks or encyclopedia entries, providing detailed descriptions nearly devoid of the author's opinion. More often, the goal is persuasion, in which the author aims to influence the audience to adopt new beliefs. Although some authors seek to recount facts impartially, even informing the audience is a kind of persuasion insofar as it causes readers to form new opinions. Persuasive passages are the most common on the MCAT; most passages on Test Day will contain at least one opinion the author tries to get the reader to endorse (with varying degrees of forcefulness). Besides altering beliefs, persuasion can also motivate individuals to take action. Such persuasion is often encountered in speeches, but it could appear on the MCAT as a set of recommendations for solving a particular problem.

Evoking an emotional response is another kind of goal, which may be distinct from persuasion. Whether the author seeks to delight the audience with humorous anecdotes or to provoke curiosity by raising unanswered questions, such a goal may be achieved by dramatically different means from those used in persuasive writing. These two categories need not be separate—certainly, an author can evoke an emotional response in an attempt to persuade the audience.

More generally, an author's **tone** helps to establish the goal of a written work. Tone reflects the author's attitude toward the subject matter. In a literary piece, the way in which the author frames the characters in the text—their personalities, dialogues, and actions—contributes to the tone. In an article, how the author describes the scenario and the individuals or entities being discussed reveals the tone. To determine tone in the text, examine the words that are used while considering the question *What imagery or feelings do these convey?*

Whether a piece is persuasive, is evocative, or serves another goal, it will invariably attempt to affect the members of an audience in some way by changing what they feel, what they believe, or what they do. Bear in mind that just as the intended audience can be misjudged, so too can the actual effect of a text depart from its author's original desires.

CONTEXT

The **context** of a written work refers to two distinct—but related—aspects of the work: the relationships among words, sentences, and paragraphs; and the larger societal situation in which the piece was written.

Bridge

Impression management, discussed in Chapter 9 of *MCAT Behavioral Sciences Review*, focuses on how we present ourselves to accomplish specific goals. Some of the impression management strategies can be employed in writing, as well, such as self-disclosure, ingratiation, and alter-casting.

Bridge

An author's Goal should be placed at the bottom of your Outline, and part of writing out that Goal is identifying the tone: is the author prescriptive? Demanding? Doubtful? Impartial? How to Outline a passage is described in Chapter 4 of *MCAT CARS Review*.

Bridge

Definition-in-Context questions, discussed in Chapter 9 of *MCAT CARS Review*, are all about your ability to ascertain the definition of a word (usually a jargon word) from its surrounding text.

Within a written work, the term *context* often refers to surrounding information. For example, the definition or intent of a word can often be discerned by reading the surrounding sentence. This approach to context can be used on a larger scale as well. The intent of a sentence can become clearer when you read the surrounding sentences, and the significance of a paragraph is dependent on the paragraphs that precede and follow it. Even a full chapter can be understood more clearly in relation to a book as a whole. Context helps with placing the author's ideas into perspective.

The term *context* can also refer to the societal situation in which the author wrote the piece. By recognizing the author, audience, and message of a piece (as well as the relationships between each), one can better understand the goal of the work. This means not only literally identifying each of these elements of the rhetorical situation but also looking beyond the pages of the text to the social, political, economic, cultural, and intellectual environment at the time. For example, *I Have a Dream* by Dr. Martin Luther King Jr. is far better understood when one considers the impetus for the civil rights movement in the early 1960s than if one reads the words without any awareness of their historical context. While the MCAT will not require you to know anything about the sociohistorical context outside of the information contained in the passage (or in the accompanying question stems), it is critical to recognize that the author's tone and voice—further illustrated in the next section—are influenced by context in this broader sense.

Let's return to why the rhetorical situation, diagrammed in Figure 2.1, is so important in medicine. Many people are interested in eating healthfully and staying fit, and many people are interested in expanding their knowledge about their bodies. However, most patients with whom you interact will not be reading the *Journal of the American Medical Association* (*JAMA*) or the *New England Journal of Medicine* (*NEJM*), which routinely publish medical studies with this information. Instead, most will find information in health and wellness magazines, in online forums, or on popular television shows. These media deliver this health information in a more understandable way for those who are not highly educated in medicine.

Medical journals and the more popular media are both intended to inform; however, one is aimed at vetting the latest research through peer review and delivering that research to health professionals, while the other presents conclusions and recommendations to the general public. The difference between these two rhetorical situations can lead to vastly different interpretations of the same research. A less-informed blogger may present faulty conclusions, a magazine partially funded by pharmaceutical companies may be biased in its descriptions of a particular medication, and a sensationalist television show may exaggerate the importance of a discovery. By recognizing the rhetorical situation in which information is presented, a physician can better understand how his patients think and can advise and work with these patients more effectively.

Figure 2.1. The Rhetorical Situation

2.3 Rhetorical Analysis

Now that we have established a common vocabulary to discuss rhetoric, let's take a look at rhetorical analysis—the application of rhetorical knowledge.

EXAMPLES

Following are three contrasting passages that demonstrate the conventions of rhetorical knowledge. All three of the passages focus on the same topic: Aristotle's *Rhetoric*.

Example Passage 1

Aristotle's brilliance is further on display in the study of rhetoric. The canonical *Rhetoric*, much in the fashion of his numerous other ground-breaking treatises, lays the foundation for an entire academic discipline, elucidating rhetoric's multifarious nature as Aristotle employs a series of clarifying distinctions. Thus, Aristotle demonstrates the vast scope of rhetoric by calling it the *antistrophe* or counterpart to *dialectic*. While the dialectician attempts to determine what is actually true or ethically good, the rhetorician tries to persuade others of the truth or goodness of something. Among his most remarkable insights is Aristotle's division of the three modes of persuasion. When an orator draws upon rational argumentation to convince an audience, he or she is employing *logos* or logical persuasion. If speakers wish to establish credibility to demonstrate that

MCAT Expertise

When you see examples like these three passages in this book, try to come up with answers on your own before looking at Kaplan's answers. In this set of examples, determine the message, voice, goal, and tone of each example. If you train yourself to think critically while you practice, it will be second nature to do so on Test Day.

they know what they're talking about and that they are not being deceptive, they use *ethos* or the ethical mode. Finally, *pathos* or emotional persuasion is utilized whenever a speaker attempts to influence the audience's feelings to incline its members to think or act in a particular way. Of course, Aristotle in his wisdom recognizes that effective oratory almost invariably displays characteristics of all three.

Example Passage 2

Another area in which Aristotle was influential is the field of rhetoric. In his book entitled *Rhetoric*, Aristotle employs his typical approach of categorization, delineating the various aspects of the subject of inquiry. According to Aristotle, rhetoric is the practical complement to the more theoretical *dialectic*: the latter concerns matters of truth and goodness while the former concerns the means of persuasion. This persuasion is accomplished by using one or more of three basic modes or methods: *logos*, *ethos*, and *pathos*. *Logos*, or logical persuasion, relies upon reason, employing both deductive proofs (*syllogisms* or *enthymemes*) and inductive inferences made through the use of examples. *Ethos*, or ethical persuasion, aims to draw upon the credibility of the speaker to establish the speaker's expertise and goodwill. Lastly, *pathos*, or pathetic persuasion, sways individuals by playing upon their emotions, putting them in the proper state of mind to form beliefs or take actions as the speaker wills. Most orators will use all three methods of persuasion but will frequently emphasize one over the others.

Example Passage 3

Despite the advances of later thinkers, Aristotle continues to have a significant impact on rhetorical studies. His *Rhetoric* is all too often cited as providing a foundation for the entire discipline, notwithstanding Aristotle's penchant for simplistic classifications. One example of such is his makeshift division of all academic disciplines into two categories: theoretical *dialectic* and practical *rhetoric*. Aristotle contends that the latter operates in only three distinct ways: *logos*, the use of reason to demonstrate to an audience the truths that dialectic purportedly uncovers; *ethos*, persuasion that exploits the speaker's apparent trustworthiness and expertise; and *pathos* or emotional manipulation of the audience. Fortunately, Aristotle does not deny common sense, granting that most persuasion is a mixture of the three—although one wonders why he does not leave open the possibility of alternative methods.

There are commonalities in the passages. All three are written in an articulate manner using advanced vocabulary, which hints that the authors are highly knowledgeable about Aristotelian classifications of rhetoric. The advanced vocabulary also signals that the passages are designed for educated audiences.

Before reading the interpretations of the three passages below, decide for yourself how the principles of rhetoric apply to each example. What message does each author give? How easy is it to discern the author's voice? What is the author's goal, and how does the tone help achieve that goal?

In the first passage, the author shows that he favors Aristotle by painting the philosopher in a positive manner: *Aristotle's brilliance*, *Among his most remarkable insights*, and *Aristotle in his wisdom* are a few examples of language by which the author reveals a positive bias toward Aristotle. While the author of the first passage explains Aristotle's philosophy to the audience, the message also includes the author's subjective views. The author's voice is clearly evident, and the tone is light, respectful, and complimentary. This type of passage would likely be found in an arts and culture publication in which the goal is to highlight or celebrate the philosopher's contributions to society.

The second passage is devoid of the author's personal views and presents the information in an objective manner. That is, the message of the second example is more purely focused on providing accurate information about the Aristotelian classifications of rhetoric, without including explicit opinion. The tone is more serious and strictly informative, and the author seems to have minimized her personal voice—or has a very dry and factual voice. This type of text may appear in an encyclopedia or perhaps a textbook in which the goal is simply to provide facts.

In contrast, the final passage is rather dismissive: *Despite the advances of later thinkers, Aristotle continues to have a significant impact*; *too often cited*; *Aristotle's penchant for simplistic classifications*; and *Fortunately, Aristotle does not deny common sense* all reveal a clear negative bias toward Aristotle. The author trivializes the contributions made by Aristotle and questions the philosopher's ideology. Such text could be an excerpt from an article in an academic journal in which the author was focusing on one of Aristotle's successors or providing criticisms of Aristotle. Either way, the tone in this piece is critical, as the author's opposition is evident; the author's voice is also obvious, as in the first example. The author's goal is unmistakably to downplay or rebut Aristotle's importance while describing the classifications in *Rhetoric*.

ARISTOTELIAN RHETORIC

We would be remiss if we did not provide our own definitions of Aristotle's rhetorical classifications after the last set of examples. According to the Greek philosopher, rhetoric relies on the communication skills of both the author of the message and the audience receiving the message. Three strategies, also called **appeals**, are used in this approach: *logos*, *ethos*, and *pathos*.

The **Aristotelian triad** has some parallels to the rhetorical triangle of author, audience, and message illustrated in Figure 2.1. For effective transmission, the message conveyed by the author needs to be logically sound and based firmly in reason. Aristotle classified *logos* as an appeal to one's logic and reasoning. The author also needs to be credible and must be presented as an ethical deliverer of the message; creating an appeal via one's credibility and trustworthiness is termed *ethos*. Lastly, the author is often more successful by appealing to the audience's emotions; such an appeal is termed *pathos*. While it is the author's role to establish the logos, ethos, and pathos of a message, the audience members are also expected to use their critical reading or listening skills and reasoning abilities to analyze the message conveyed by the author.

When reading MCAT passages, it is important to consider the frame of mind of the author and his or her intent in writing the passage. This perspective gives insight into how an author uses rhetorical strategies to appeal to the audience. *Logos* in particular is especially question-worthy, so logical reasoning is addressed further in Chapters 5 and 6 of *MCAT CARS Review*.

Conclusion

All of the questions in CARS are associated with passages that you must read critically. But, as described earlier, most questions will go beyond simply comprehending the words the author says (the message) and will instead focus on higher-level concerns. What does the author's tone reveal about her opinions? How does the author's voice reflect her identity and intended audience? What is the author's goal in writing the passage? Questions like these, which reflect the underlying principles of rhetoric itself, are often encountered on Test Day.

Of course, rhetoric is not just an antiquated discipline passed down from the ancient Greeks, nor is rhetorical analysis a skill you will apply only on the MCAT. You will use these same ideas and techniques on a daily basis in medical school and as a physician. In medical school, you will learn not only the language of medicine but also the rhetorical devices used by physicians—that is, how to author a patient note that seamlessly guides other physicians to the same diagnosis as you. *A 75-year-old woman with a history of Factor V Leiden presents on post-operative day #5 status post right hip replacement with swelling of the right leg, acute onset of shortness of breath, and chest pain*—from this one sentence, a doctor is able to communicate the same message to any other physician who reads the note: *I think this woman has a deep venous thrombosis (DVT), which has sent a piece of the clot to her lungs.*

With the expansion of evidence-based medicine, you'll answer clinical questions through a meticulous analysis of the research on the topic: *Which breast cancer screening guidelines should I follow?* you may ask yourself. *Do I opt for the United States Preventive Services Task Force (USPSTF), which tends to be more conservative with screening, or the American Cancer Society (ACS), which is more rigorous? Or what about the American Congress of Obstetricians and Gynecologists (ACOG), which is somewhere in between?* An effective physician would read each group's recommendations with an eye toward the identity of each group (the authors) and each group's goals. Examples such as these make it clear that understanding rhetoric is indispensible to success on the MCAT, in medical school, and beyond.

CONCEPT AND STRATEGY SUMMARY

What Is Rhetoric?

- **Rhetoric** is the art of communicating through writing and speaking.

- **Rhetorical knowledge** refers to an awareness of the components of a written work besides the actual words on the page, such as the author, intended audience, and goal.

- **Rhetorical analysis** is the examination of a particular work for the sake of identifying its rhetorical elements (the components of rhetorical knowledge).

Key Components of Rhetoric

- The **author** is the individual writing the piece.

  - Authors who are expert on a topic, and who are writing for knowledgeable audiences, may use **jargon**, which is vocabulary specific to a particular field.

  - An author may use more Extreme keywords if he is passionate about the topic at hand. An author may use more Moderating keywords if he is less invested.

  - An author may modify his voice if writing on behalf of a group.

- The **audience** refers to the person or persons the author intended to read or hear the work.

- The **message** is the actual text written by the author, including factual information and explicit opinions.

  - The author's **voice** refers to how she uniquely strings words together to deliver a message. It is how an author expresses her thoughts and can be unique and identifiable.

  - The **genre** is the category into which the written work can be classified, such as a book, article, essay, letter, and so on.

  - The **medium** is the delivery system into which the written work can be placed, such as print, broadcast, and digital media.

- The **goal** is the reason why the author wrote the work.

  - The goal of many passages on the MCAT is to be persuasive, that is, to convince the reader to adopt new beliefs or to take action.

  - Other passages may have a goal of evoking an emotional response.

  - The author's **tone** is indicative of the goal of a written work because it reflects the author's attitude toward the subject matter.

  - Authors may write with more than one goal in mind.

- **Context** refers to two different (but related) concepts within rhetoric.

  - ○ Within a written work, context refers to surrounding material that can be used to figure out the definition or significance of a particular element in the work. For example, a word's definition may be inferred from the other words in the same sentence; a paragraph's importance can be determined by comparison with nearby paragraphs.

  - ○ Context can also refer to the greater social, political, economic, cultural, and intellectual environment in which the work was written.

Rhetorical Analysis

- Rhetoric depends on the communication skills of both the author of the message and the audience receiving the message.

- The **Aristotelian triad** describes three strategies or appeals used by an author to effectively transmit his message.

  - ○ *Logos*, or logical persuasion, appeals to the audience's rational judgment. *Ethos*, or ethical persuasion, appeals via the author's credibility.

  - ○ *Pathos*, or emotional persuasion, appeals to the audience's feelings.

3

Keywords

In This Chapter

Introduction

One of the biggest mistakes you can make as a student is to think that learning how to read is a one-time occurrence, like a switch that, once flipped, fully illuminates the darkened recesses of illiteracy and ignorance. In truth, it is always possible to improve your ability to read, both by refining your current approach and by broadening your capacity to read a range of texts in a variety of settings. Would you read a novel for pleasure the same way you read a textbook for homework? Once you recognize that there are many ways to read and multiple levels on which the written word can be appreciated, then you can learn to customize your reading approach to fit your particular purpose, whether it be relaxing with a piece of fiction or reaching for that higher score on the MCAT!

In this chapter, you'll learn new ways to read strategically by paying attention to special terms that we call **keywords**. We begin with a discussion of how to read using these vital clues before examining each of the three major categories in turn. First, Relation keywords highlight the connections between ideas in passages: similarities, differences, and other relationships. Next, Author keywords are vital for providing insight into the mind of the passage's author. Finally, Logic keywords elucidate the reasoning in a text, which is the most frequently tested aspect of passages in the *Critical Analysis and Reasoning Skills* (CARS) section. In the chapter that follows, the discussion of keywords will continue as their place in the Kaplan Method for CARS Passages is explained and demonstrated through the analysis of an example CARS passage, so treat Chapter 4 of *MCAT CARS Review* as a companion to this one.

Key Concept

Keywords are words and phrases commonly employed in CARS passages that serve as valuable clues for answering the accompanying questions. They fall into three broad categories: Relation, Author, and Logic.

3.1 Reading Strategically with Keywords

When it comes to reading dense academic prose—and this describes just about every passage in the CARS section—there are at least four ways to approach the text; that is, there are four distinct levels on which it might be appreciated. The first of these modes, **content**, is what you're most likely accustomed to looking for, whether reading for work or leisure. On Test Day, you will want to pay attention to informational content, but you'll also want to broaden your focus to encompass the other three modes of reading: for **organization**, **perspective**, and **reasoning**.

READ FOR CONTENT

Reading for content simply involves extracting the information from the text, discovering precisely *what* is being said. This is akin to looking for the message of the passage, as described in Chapter 2 of *MCAT CARS Review*. It is important to note that you will never be expected to have preexisting familiarity with the content of a passage in the CARS section; all information necessary to answer the questions is contained within the content of the passage itself. This is in stark contrast to passages in the three science sections, in which you are expected to integrate outside knowledge with new information provided in the passage.

When reading for content, ask yourself questions like *What is the author saying? What is the main idea of this passage? What topics are being explored? What opinions has the author stated in the passage?* We will not discuss specific lists of keywords when reading for content; instead, we will focus on **buzzwords**, as we do in the sciences. Buzzwords include proper nouns, names, dates, new terms, and jargon.

READ FOR ORGANIZATION

Although there are many ways to talk about the "organization" of a passage, we are specifically referring to the ways in which the different ideas presented in the passage relate to one another. If the informational content is the *what* of the text, then the organization is the *how*. As you'll see in the next chapter, this organizational structure will be reflected in the Outline you construct on your scratch paper, as you Label each paragraph to account for its function within the larger passage.

As you read for organization, you'll be considering questions like the following: *How does what I'm reading now connect to what came before? How many distinct ideas are actually being presented in this paragraph? Is this a new concept or just a restatement of a previous one? Where is the author going with this? How does this new point connect to the author's thesis?* Answering these questions becomes much more manageable when authors use Relation keywords. You may have learned about these in high school English or freshman composition courses as "transition words" because they facilitate the movement (or transition) between sentences.

READ FOR PERSPECTIVE

In addition to watching out for the organization of ideas, you'll also want to pay attention to the different perspectives contained in the passage. Many authors of the passages used in CARS attempt to conceal their biases and mask their opinions as facts; they rarely state their intentions overtly. Therefore, it is essential to attend to the rhetorical aspects of the text presented in Chapter 2 of *MCAT CARS Review*, especially the goal, tone, and voice. The key to reading for perspective is thinking about the *why* behind the *how*. Consider the author's Goal in writing the passage and how each part of the passage functions in achieving that larger objective.

While every text embodies its author's perspective, many passages contain alternative voices as well, often noted by references to particular thinkers like *Carol Gilligan* or *Ludwig Wittgenstein* or to schools of thought like *postmodernism* or *American pragmatism*. On other occasions, divergent perspectives are indicated more indirectly by reference to a *traditional view* or *critics* or, even more subtly, with language like *some contend* or *others have argued*. In passages that feature multiple viewpoints, you are virtually guaranteed to see questions that require you to sort out *who* exactly said *what*.

Reading for perspective means thinking about the following: *Why is the author writing this? What is the purpose of this part of the passage? How many distinct voices are there in the passage? Does the author agree with what is said in this sentence, or does this sentence represent some other voice? How does the author really feel about this?* The second type of keywords, called Author keywords, thrust you inside the mind of the writer, letting you see things from her perspective.

READ FOR REASONING

Finally, the fourth way to read a passage is to examine the structure of its reasoning. In just about every passage that you'll encounter on Test Day, the author will attempt to persuade the audience to adopt certain beliefs. To do so, it's not enough simply to repeat the claim that she wants you to accept. Rather, the author provides supporting reasons, or additional statements that make those beliefs more plausible. Giving reasons is also known as arguing, argumentation, or making an argument—what we called *logos* or logical appeals in the preceding chapter. You'll find that the logical structure of a text might be quite different from its organization: for instance, the so-called "conclusion" of the author's main argument could come in the first sentence of the passage.

While reading for reasoning, ask yourself questions like: *What is the author trying to convince the audience to believe? Are there any reasons given to believe this sentence is true? Does this new claim make a previous one more plausible, or does it perhaps challenge an earlier one? What evidence or refutations does the author provide for this opinion? Which claims in the passage are given the most support?* The final keyword category, Logic, will aid you in sorting out the structure of the argument. Furthermore, argumentation and logic are such crucial topics for Test Day that they constitute the focus of both Chapters 5 and 6 of *MCAT CARS Review*—a necessary supplement to the discussion of Logic keywords below.

3.2 Relation Keywords

When tackling a CARS passage, it is essential to be able to understand how what you're reading now fits into the whole—what we just called reading for organization. While there are many ways in which ideas might be related to one another, the vast majority of **Relation keywords** will fall into one of two subcategories: Similarity or Difference.

SIMILARITY

Keywords that indicate relations of similarity include *and, also, moreover, furthermore*, and so on. In addition, phrases that indicate examples (*such as, for instance*, and *take the case of*) fall into this category, as do demonstrative pronouns (*this, that, these, those*). Generally speaking, when a sentence or clause begins with a **Similarity keyword**, it will be continuing in the same vein as what came before. In other words, it won't be saying anything particularly new. As a consequence, if you understood the preceding material, you can generally read a clause that follows a Similarity keyword quickly, briskly moving through the text until a new keyword signals something different. On the other hand, if you struggled to understand a particular sentence but see a Similarity keyword at the beginning of the next sentence, keep moving forward—the author is likely to continue with the same idea but may rephrase it in easier words.

Even though they are not technically key*words*, certain punctuation marks can also indicate a similar idea is coming up. Most notably, colons (:) and semicolons (;) are commonly employed to function as the verbal equivalent of the equal sign (=). The use of dashes—such as the ones surrounding this clause—and parentheses (the marks enclosing this phrase) also tend to indicate elaboration upon the same general theme. Finally, keep an eye out for quotation marks (" and "): while quotes can serve a variety of functions, one of the most common is to use another person's voice to restate the point the author just made.

MCAT Expertise

If you understand what an author is saying and encounter a Similarity keyword, skim the following text. You know you'll be seeing more of the same idea, and you may save a few seconds of time—those seconds add up!

DIFFERENCE

In contrast, **Difference keywords** will usually merit additional attention when you encounter them because they tend to suggest more interesting (and therefore testable) relationships than similarity or continuity. Common Difference keywords like *but*, *yet*, *however*, *although*, and *otherwise* signal a change in the direction of the text. Like Similarity keywords, Difference words serve as transitions between sentences, but they can also indicate deeper conceptual relations—the differences between two solutions to a political problem, a point of disagreement between various critics of a literary work, or a rapid change in opinion from one time period to another, to give just a few examples. The connections between ideas are among the most commonly tested aspects of CARS passages, so strive to understand these relationships with as much specificity as the clues given allow.

While punctuation symbols often indicate similarity, this is not always true. If a punctuation symbol is accompanied by another type of keyword, the actual word or phrase generally takes precedence in determining the relationship (for example, a semicolon followed by *yet* usually suggests a point of difference rather than similarity). This points out the greater importance of anticipating while you read; a great score in CARS is predicated on your ability to be a critical reader rather than a passive reader. When we passively read for pleasure, we tend to glide over text and often only understand the superficial message of the written work. In critical reading, we are continuously questioning the text and setting expectations for where the author will go with an idea. Even if they are not met, it is still worthwhile to set these expectations. In fact, when an author takes a starkly different route in a part of the passage than we expect, the testmakers are more likely to ask about this text. That which is rhetorically unusual in the passage and frustrates expectations becomes excellent material for MCAT questions.

MORE COMPLEX RELATIONSHIPS

While the keywords considered under this heading might broadly count as Difference keywords, they designate special types of divergence and are especially ripe for CARS questions. While by no means exhaustive of the types of relations you might see on Test Day, Oppositions, Sequences, and Comparisons are three of the most common.

Oppositions

Words like *not*, *never*, *on the contrary*, and *as opposed to* indicate not merely a difference but an outright **Opposition** or conflict between ideas. Many CARS authors like to create **dichotomies**, which are divisions of entities into two categories. These categories are considered **mutually exclusive**, meaning that they don't overlap. The use of *either … or*, *on one hand … on the other hand*, and

MCAT Expertise

When you encounter a Difference keyword, slow down your reading slightly. These keywords signify a change in the author's focus or a direct contrast between two things; either way, we need to know how the trajectory of the passage is changing to keep a step ahead of the author.

Bridge

Mutual exclusivity is also an important condition in some probability problems. If two potential outcomes are mutually exclusive, the probability of both occurring, $P(A \text{ and } B) = 0$. If they are also exhaustive, then the probability of either occurring, $P(A \text{ or } B) = 1$. Probability rules are discussed in Chapter 12 of *MCAT Physics and Math Review*.

similar parallel phrase constructions are good indications of a **dualism**. Often, but not always, these dichotomies will be depicted as **exhaustive**, meaning that everything falls into one of the two categories. For example, an author writing about human behavior might claim that *all actions are either free choices or involuntary reflexes*, leaving no space for shades of gray.

Sequences

Some Relation keywords suggest a series of events advancing in time: *initially, first, second, third, next, subsequently, before, after, last, finally.* These words will usually be spaced relatively evenly throughout the passage or at least throughout a paragraph or two, so note how they organize the text into chunks. **Sequences** are something of a hybrid between Similarity and Difference, with each word suggesting not only a connection to a larger process but also a departure from the other steps in the series. Generally, you're better off taking your time with these, at least until you have a good idea of how the sequence will unfold.

Some sequences can set up a clear difference between time periods. *Historically, traditionally, used to, originally,* and—when used in comparison to a later time—*initially* and *before* can be used as time-based Difference keywords when contrasted with words like *now, currently, modern, later,* and *after*. Such a setup often implies that new information was learned or discovered in the intervening time: *The traditional interpretation vs. a more modern understanding* or *Historically, we thought vs. But now, we know.*

Comparisons

Sometimes authors will evaluate ideas and rank them relative to other ideas. More often than not, authors will consider only two concepts at a time, contrasting them through the use of **Comparison keywords** like *more, less, better,* and *worse.* That said, occasionally authors will compare three or more items, or offer vague judgments of superiority (or inferiority) of one item over all others, reflected by superlatives such as *most, least, best,* and *worst.* When revealing attitudes, Comparison keywords function more like Author keywords, further explained below.

Table 3.1 lists examples of Relation keywords in each category. Note that some words can fit into more than one category; for example, *not* reveals a difference, but it can also indicate a direct opposition.

Similarity	Difference	Opposition
and	but	not/never/none
also	yet	either … or
moreover	however	as opposed to
furthermore	although	on the contrary
like	(even) though	versus (*vs.*)
same/similar	rather (than)	on one hand … on the other hand
that is	in contrast	otherwise
in other words	on the other hand	**Sequence**
for example	otherwise	before/after
take the case of	nevertheless	earlier/later
for instance	whereas	previous/next
including	while	initially/subsequently/finally
such as	different	first/second/third/last
in addition	unlike	historically/traditionally/used to
plus	notwithstanding	now/currently/modern
at the same time	another	**Comparison**
as well as	instead	better/best
equally	still	worse/worst
this/that/these/those	despite	less/least
: [colon]	alternatively	more/most
; [semicolon]	unless	*–er/–est*
— [dash]	not	primarily
( ) [parentheses]	conversely	especially
" " [quotes]	contrarily	above all

Table 3.1. Common Relation Keywords

MCAT Expertise

Simply memorizing lists of keywords is not sufficient to extract all the information from a passage. A Difference keyword can serve slightly different functions depending on the context in which the word is found. An Evidence keyword may actually provide very little support for the logic of a passage, depending on how the author structures her argument. Recognize that MCAT CARS success is not about memorizing the fact that *but*, *yet*, and *however* are Difference keywords but instead understanding how Difference keywords affect our interpretation of the author's message.

3.3 Author Keywords

Author keywords can be among the most subtle clues that you'll encounter on Test Day, but they are crucial for answering the many questions you'll face that ask about the author's attitudes. Authors of passages used in CARS rarely say *I believe* or *it seems to me* (and if you do find this language, it's more often in the humanities than the social sciences). Instead, they are more likely to hint at their opinions by selecting verbs, nouns, adjectives, and adverbs that carry a particular emotional valence— a connotation of either approval or disapproval. Moreover, authors will use characteristic words and short phrases to make their claims more Extreme (indicating emphasis and strengthening ideas), as well as others that Moderate their claims (qualifying or limiting what they are saying and weakening ideas).

POSITIVE *vs.* NEGATIVE

Understanding the author's attitude becomes a much simpler matter if we employ a metaphor taken from the sciences. Just as an atom or molecule might possess an electrostatic charge, so too can a word or phrase contain a kind of emotional charge that may be positive or negative. Because most of the language in CARS passages tends to be "uncharged" or neutral, you'll predominantly pay attention to the exceptions—those cases in which terms have clear positive or negative connotations.

Positive keywords include nouns such as *masterpiece*, *genius*, and *triumph*; verbs such as *excel*, *succeed*, and *know*; adjectives such as *compelling*, *impressive*, and *elegant*; and adverbs such as *correctly*, *reasonably*, and *fortunately*. Among **Negative keywords** would be nouns such as *disaster*, *farce*, and *limitation*; verbs such as *miss*, *fail*, and *confuse*; adjectives such as *problematic*, *so-called*, and *deceptive*; and adverbs such as *questionably*, *merely*, and *purportedly*.

Keep in mind that, just as there is a difference between a cation with a +1 charge and one with a +3 charge, so too is there a difference between a moderately positive opinion and an extremely positive one. For instance, an author probably approves more strongly of a novelist described as *a masterful artist* than one portrayed merely as *a decent writer*. Consequently, it may be helpful to think of the author's attitude as varying along a spectrum or continuum, with extremely positive opinions on the one end and extremely negative on the other, as in Figure 3.1. Note that most authors' attitudes in CARS fall in a comfortable middle ground between being too extreme and being too moderate, as implied by the relative widths of the sections in the diagram. When Outlining a passage, as described in Chapter 4 of *MCAT CARS Review*, the author's attitude can be written in shorthand: + for moderately positive, − − − for extremely negative, and so on.

Figure 3.1. The Spectrum of Author Attitudes (Linear)

Note that in addition to positive, negative, or neutral, an author can also be **ambivalent**. Ambivalence literally means *feeling both ways*, and it is as different from **impartiality**—having no strong opinion one way or another—as the set of 1 and −1 is from the number 0. Continuing the analogy with electrostatic charge, an ambivalent attitude is like an amino acid in its *zwitterionic* form, with both a positively charged and a negatively charged end, and an impartial attitude is like an uncharged, unpolarized atom. Describing the net zero charge of a zwitterion as merely "neutral" would mean neglecting its distinctive properties. The MCAT won't let you get away with such oversimplifications!

EXTREME

Placing a particular idea on the author-attitude spectrum above becomes easier by paying attention to **Extreme keywords**, a type of Author keyword that you can imagine as enhancing the charge of what the author is saying, forcing the author into one or the other extreme. These words and short phrases are functionally equivalent to exclamation points (!), offering insight into what the author feels passionately about and regards as important.

Examples of Extreme keywords include *indeed*, *very*, *really*, *quite*, *primarily*, *especially*, *obviously*, *foremost*, *always*, *in fact*, *above all*, and *it is clear that*. Note that words that indicate necessity, like *need* and *must*, also serve as Extreme keywords, as do words that indicate value judgments like *should* and *ought*—these tend to be rare in CARS passages, so they deserve special consideration.

MODERATING

Authors will sometimes modify the strength of their claims in the other direction by using qualifying language, also known as *hedging*. **Moderating keywords** are those words that set limits on claims in order to make them easier to support because a stronger statement is always more difficult to prove than a weaker one. So, to consider one example, it would be an extreme claim to say that *human beings are only motivated by greed*. Though some might agree with this formulation, the bulk of MCAT authors would sooner water it down by saying something like *in many aspects of life, humans are predominantly motivated by greed*, or even further limit it to a subset of human beings, such as *investment bankers are often motivated by greed*. Such modifications transform a controversial claim into one that is much more plausible.

Among the most important Moderating keywords are those that use the language of possibility, such as *can*, *could*, *may*, and *might*. Claims about what is possible are always weaker than claims about what is definitely true. Other Moderating keywords include limits on time or place, whether stated specifically or in vague phrases such as *now*, *here*, *at times*, *in some cases*, or *in this instance*. Still others will impose general constraints on meaning; examples include *in this sense*, *according to this interpretation*, or *in a manner of speaking*.

Key Concept

While they are both neutral overall, these two attitudes are very different:
- Ambivalent = having both a positive and negative opinion
- Impartial = having neither a positive nor negative opinion

ACCOUNTING FOR OPPOSITION

One final consideration when working with Author keywords is contradiction or opposition, a special type of Difference mentioned above. It can be particularly tricky to figure out authors' attitudes in CARS when they use double negatives (or worse!). The key is to remember that the opposite of an extreme statement will typically be a moderate statement of the reverse charge. In the diagram below, which is just a slight rearrangement of the author attitude spectrum presented in Figure 3.1, a word of opposition will typically serve to flip the author's view 180 degrees.

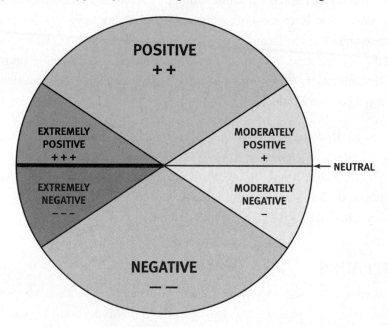

Figure 3.2. The Spectrum of Author Attitudes (Circular)

So, if an author were to claim that a particular event is *impossible*, this statement would fall somewhere in the extremely negative range. On the other hand, suggesting the situation was *not impossible* would be making a moderately positive claim, effectively saying that it was *possible*. Be aware, however, that some words retain their strength even when accompanied with *not* or some other word of opposition—for instance, *must* is extremely positive in charge, while *must not* is extremely negative in charge.

Table 3.2 lists examples of Author keywords in each category.

Positive	Negative	Extreme	Moderating
masterpiece	disaster	must	can/could
genius	farce	need/necessary	may/might
triumph	limitation	always	possibly
excel	miss	every	probably
succeed	fail	any	sometimes
know	confuse	only	on occasion
compelling	problematic	should/ought	often
impressive	so-called	indeed	tends to
elegant	deceptive	very	here
correctly	questionably	especially	now
reasonably	merely	obviously	in this case
fortunately	purportedly	above all	in some sense

Table 3.2. Common Author Keywords

3.4 Logic Keywords

The final level of reading (for reasoning) is perhaps the most difficult because the special one-way relationship between a conclusion and its evidence is among the most complex you'll encounter on Test Day. Making matters worse is that **Logic keywords** tend to be relatively rare, occurring less frequently than either Relation or Author keywords in most passages. As a final complication, when they do occur, they are sometimes used to refer to causal connections rather than logical justifications. Notwithstanding these difficulties, Logic keywords are a powerful tool: once you gain proficiency in recognizing them and understanding what they entail, you'll find the many CARS questions on reasoning much less daunting.

EVIDENCE AND CONCLUSION

The precise nature of the relationship between the different parts of an argument will be considered in Chapter 6 of *MCAT CARS Review*, but for now you can use the following simple distinction: a **conclusion** is a claim that the author (or whomever the author is speaking for) is trying to convince the audience to believe, while pieces of **evidence** are the reasons that are given for believing it. Be sure to determine whenever you see the following keywords whether the conclusion is one that the author would endorse or whether it is intended to represent some other viewpoint by paying attention to nearby Author keywords and other clues.

Typical examples of **Evidence keywords** are *because, since, if, why, the reason is, on account of, due to, as a result of, is justified by,* and *after all*. There is a bit less

MCAT Expertise

Having trouble figuring out what part of the argument a Logic keyword is indicating? Try this simple substitution test: if you can replace the word or phrase with *because* or *because of,* then whatever follows is a piece of evidence. If, instead, *therefore* would preserve the meaning, the subsequent claim is a conclusion.

variety in **Conclusion keywords**, which also tend to occur less frequently than Evidence keywords. The most important conclusion words to know are *therefore*, *thus*, *then*, *so*, *consequently*, *leading to*, *resulting in*, *argue*, and *conclude*.

In Chapter 6 of *MCAT CARS Review*, the exact nature of logical support, also known as **justification**, will be discussed in depth. However, it's important to note that Evidence and Conclusion keywords sometimes signal a different relationship: cause and effect. Unlike a mere correlation, in which two occurrences are found to accompany one another, **causation** is a one-way relationship in which the first event (cause) always precedes the second (effect). Moreover, in contrast to sequences of events, which may happen coincidentally, causes are directly responsible for leading to their effects. The upshot of this is that whenever you encounter Evidence or Conclusion keywords, you should always clarify whether you are dealing with events in the world that have causal connections or with statements about the world that have logical ones.

REFUTATION

Refutation keywords will not always be included in the presentation of an argument, but they are effectively the opposite of evidence—countervailing reasons for rejecting a conclusion. Although rarer than other Logic keywords, Refutation keywords are important when they do occur for representing one of the most commonly tested aspects of logical reasoning. They include words such as *despite*, *notwithstanding*, *challenge*, *object*, *counter*, *critique*, *conflict*, and *problem*.

Table 3.3 lists examples of Logic keywords in each category.

Evidence	Conclusion	Refutation
because (of)	therefore	despite
since	thus	notwithstanding
if	then	challenge
for	so	undermined by
why	consequently	object
the reason is	leading to	counter(argument)
as a result of	resulting in	critique/criticize
due to	argue	conflict
as evident in	conclude	doubt
justified by	imply	problem
assuming	infer	weakness
after all	suggest	called into question by

Table 3.3. Common Logic Keywords

Conclusion

By watching out for Relation, Author, and Logic keywords, you'll find yourself appreciating the text on multiple levels, going beyond the content to look at organization, perspective, and reasoning. In the subsequent chapter, we'll expand on the ideas introduced here, discussing in depth how you can use the insights gained from strategic reading to construct a scratch paper Outline of the passage, Labeling what is vital in each paragraph to make answering the questions more efficient.

CONCEPT AND STRATEGY SUMMARY

Reading Strategically with Keywords

- **Keywords** help us figure out how information is related within a passage, or they may modify our interpretation of the text around them.

- When we read for content, we ask *What does the text say?*

  ○ Reading for content is guided by buzzwords, like proper nouns, names, dates, new terms, and jargon.

  ○ You are never expected to have prior familiarity with the content of a passage in CARS.

- When we read for organization, we ask *How do sentences connect?* and *How do ideas relate?*

  ○ Reading for organization is guided by **Relation keywords**.

  ○ The organizational structure of a passage should be Outlined on scratch paper.

- When we read for perspective, we ask *Why does the author write? How does the author feel?* and *Who else has a voice?*

  ○ Reading for perspective is guided by **Author keywords**.

  ○ Other individuals' voices can be referred to specifically (by name, by category) or vaguely (*some* or *others*).

- When we read for reasoning, we ask *How are claims supported?* and *How are claims challenged?*

  ○ Reading for reasoning is guided by **Logic keywords**.

  ○ The logical structure of a passage may be quite different from its organization.

Relation Keywords

- Relation keywords show how what you're reading now fits into the passage as a whole.

- **Similarity keywords** indicate that the following material continues in the same vein as the preceding material.

- **Difference keywords** signal a change in the trajectory of the passage.

- **Opposition keywords** are particularly strong Difference keywords that create a dichotomy, or divisions of entities into two categories.

  ○ **Mutually exclusive** categories do not overlap.

  ○ When dichotomies are **exhaustive**, all relevant entities fit into one or the other category.

- **Sequence keywords** suggest a series of events advancing in time. They may also be used to set up a contrast between two time periods.
- **Comparison keywords** rank ideas relative to each other.

Author Keywords

- Author keywords indicate the author's thoughts or opinions about the topic.
- **Positive** and **Negative keywords** indicate whether an author likes, agrees with, or supports the topic; dislikes, disagrees with, or opposes the topic. Authors can also be neutral.
  - An author with an **ambivalent** attitude has both positive and negative opinions on a topic.
  - An author with an **impartial** attitude has neither positive nor negative opinions on a topic.
- **Extreme keywords** enhance the charge of what the author is saying.
- **Moderating keywords** permit the author to qualify a claim, or hedge.
- The opposite of an extreme statement tends to be a moderate statement with the opposite charge.

Logic Keywords

- Logic keywords indicate the relationships between different parts of a logical argument.
- **Conclusion keywords** signal what the author is trying to convince the audience to believe.
- **Evidence keywords** describe the reasons why the audience should believe the author's claim.
- **Refutation keywords** provide reasons for rejecting a conclusion.

Outlining the Passage

In This Chapter

Introduction

Great writers work with a plan. If you've ever had to construct an outline for homework as part of a larger essay assignment, your teacher was trying to impart to you this piece of wisdom. By forcing you to clarify your thesis and to articulate in just a few words what each paragraph is supposed to accomplish, outlining your paper typically makes writing itself much more streamlined, a simple matter of filling in the details to support your main points. On Test Day, your task will be to apply this insight by working backward, getting inside the mind of the author to reverse-engineer an outline that he could have used to compose the passage. As you'll soon discover, the process of constructing a Passage Outline sufficiently prepares you to answer the accompanying questions, and serves as a valuable resource for efficiently navigating the text to score points quickly.

The plan for this chapter is as follows: first, we take a look at the four-step Kaplan Method for Passages, called **Outlining**. The same method applies to science passages as well, but we'll examine how each of the steps is applied specifically in the *Critical Analysis and Reasoning Skills* (CARS) section. In the subsequent section, we discuss the hands-on approach to use on Test Day to construct your Outline with maximal efficiency, given the computer-based test format and limited scratch paper. We conclude the chapter with an opportunity for you to practice the Kaplan Method for CARS Passages using a full-size passage and to evaluate your performance by comparing your process and results to our examples.

4.1 The Kaplan Method for CARS Passages

Great test takers also work with a plan! Figure 4.1 shows the Kaplan Method for CARS Passages. We recommend following these four steps whenever approaching an MCAT passage.

Figure 4.1. The Kaplan Method for Passages

While this general strategy is universal, it can be refined to fit the section that you're working on. As you've probably already discovered, there are several important differences between passages from the three science sections and those found in CARS. Most obvious is that the latter contain considerably more words, as well as having no images to break up the monotony of text. Going past the surface, CARS passages are much more variable, both in their range of topics and their diversity of writing styles. Moreover, unlike the science passages, which are nearly always impartial, CARS passages are usually written by authors who take sides and express their opinions, although not always in a straightforward manner.

To account for these essential differences, the Kaplan Method for CARS Passages can be refined as shown in Figure 4.2.

SCAN FOR STRUCTURE
- Look for the big picture
- Assess the relative difficulty
- Decide to read *now* or *later*

READ STRATEGICALLY
- Read for organization—Relation keywords
- Read for perspective—Author keywords
- Read for reasoning—Logic keywords

LABEL EACH COMPONENT
- Briefly outline the function of each paragraph
- Tag author opinions and alternative voices
- Note where to find evidence and refutations

REFLECT ON YOUR OUTLINE
- Ask: informative or persuasive?
- Choose a purpose verb
- Record the author's Goal

Figure 4.2. The Kaplan Method for Passages in CARS

Note: The Kaplan Method for CARS Passages, as well as the Kaplan Method for CARS Questions, CARS Question Types, and Wrong Answer Pathologies are included as tear-out sheets in the back of this book.

SCAN

The purpose of the **Scan** step is to give you an idea of what you're getting into, to allow you to decide whether this is the passage that you want to work on at this point in time. Scanning should only take a matter of seconds and is finished when you can answer the question: *Now or later?* If your answer is *now*, you'll continue with the other steps in the method. Should you instead decide *later*, you may wish to take a few seconds to jot down on your scratch paper the topic of the passage and the number of its first question for reference, then move on to Scan the next passage.

Scanning passages is trickier in CARS than in the other sections, given the lack of figures with helpful captions—or anything besides paragraphs of text. Your best bet is to Scan for words that stand out due to capitalization, italics, quotation marks, parentheses, or any other distinctive textual features. When in doubt, just read the first (and possibly last) sentences of each paragraph until you start to get a sense of the big picture: the field of study, topic or theme, and rhetorical features like the author's purpose for writing. Remember that you don't need to read sentences word for word while Scanning: you're just trying to get enough information to assess the difficulty.

The *now* or *later* decision ultimately comes down to your individual talents as a test-taker. If you find that, say, technical philosophy passages take you a long time to complete with little payoff, then you'll want to save any such passages until the end. Why waste precious minutes on a difficult passage if filling in guesses would result in a similar score on that passage? Remember to pay attention not only to the subject matter but also to the difficulty of the language used. Puzzling vocabulary, convoluted sentences, and endless paragraphs can make even the most interesting topics frustrating to read. With enough practice, making determinations of difficulty will come quickly, and the small amount of time you invest in Scanning will pay off in points through better section management.

READ

Reading strategically means paying attention to keywords and the four modes of reading discussed in the preceding chapter: *content*, *organization*, *perspective*, and *reasoning*. Look beyond the content **buzzwords** to see how **Relation keywords** connect the different ideas in the text, how **Author keywords** offer glimpses of the writer's intentions, and how **Logic keywords** reveal the passage's arguments. If you don't yet feel comfortable identifying the different types of keywords, the analysis of the sample passage at the end of this chapter offers many examples that demonstrate how to recognize them.

Bridge

Make sure to familiarize yourself with the different types of keywords and their functions. Keywords help you anticipate the path an author will take through the passage, and they allow you stay a step ahead of the author's thought process. Chapter 3 of *MCAT CARS Review* discusses the different classifications of keywords.

As you read through each paragraph, you must resist the urge to reread the text excessively: you don't need to understand every single word and clause so long as you get a sense of the general direction of the author's discussion. A good rule of thumb is never to read a sentence more than twice during the Read step. If you don't understand a phrase or sentence the first time through, check whether a Relation keyword starts the next sentence—especially a **Similarity keyword**. If you see a Similarity keyword, it suggests that the author will continue with the same train of thought; often, the author will use simpler text to clarify the point made in preceding convoluted or complex sentences. Even if you feel lost after a second reading of the phrase or sentence, keep moving forward. You can always come back to that text for additional rereading if a question actually asks about it and points are on the line.

Above all, aim to figure out how a paragraph's sentences work together and what specific role that paragraph plays in the larger whole of the passage. The sooner you can figure out the author's overall purpose for writing, the easier it will be to see how each paragraph is supposed to function. That's why it's so helpful during the Scan step to look for those big-picture rhetorical elements (author, audience, message, goal, and context).

LABEL

The only components a CARS passage contains are paragraphs of text, so you'll be jotting down a brief description for each paragraph based on the results of your strategic reading during the **Label** step. Because you are the only person who needs to be able to decipher your Outline, you should strive to be efficient by using symbols, abbreviations, and other shorthand. Although Outlining will be a time-consuming process when you start practicing, you'll soon find a balance between being quick and being thorough. Like the Scan step, Labeling is a time investment. But because it will save you a considerable amount of effort when it comes to researching the questions, you'll find it becomes a net time *gain* once you've mastered Outlining.

Whenever possible, you should Label a paragraph in light of the four modes of reading discussed in Chapter 3 of *MCAT CARS Review*: content, organization, perspective, and reasoning. Not only should your Label reveal the content of that paragraph, but it should also give a sense of the paragraph's function within the larger structure of the passage, that is, the author's purpose for the particular paragraph. Make note in your Label of strong author opinions, as well as whenever an alternative perspective is being spoken for. Finally, pay special attention to the use of supporting or challenging evidence—many paragraphs function simply to strengthen or weaken a particular claim. Examples of each of these considerations will be offered later in this chapter.

It's essential to note that Reading and Labeling happen simultaneously. You should not start reading a new paragraph until you have some kind of Label for the one that you've just finished. Typically, it's worth reading the entire paragraph first before writing anything down because that tends to minimize the need for modifying your Label if the paragraph takes an unexpected turn. However, if the paragraph is especially long or dense, you might want to start jotting down a few words as soon as you get an idea of what's going on. Then, once you reach the end of the paragraph, just be sure your Label captures everything you feel is important before continuing.

It is worth saying that a Label in your Outline is not simply a set of notes. Writing out long lists of notes reduces the utility of your Outline because there is far too much detail for it to serve as a quick reference or guide to the passage as a whole. Further, taking notes usually accompanies a focus on content alone, rather than considering the larger function of the paragraph. Instead, a Label should be a brief summary of the paragraph as a whole, simultaneously encompassing the content, organization, perspective, and reasoning within that paragraph.

REFLECT

With each paragraph now Read and Labeled, all that remains is to pause briefly to **Reflect** upon the whole passage and articulate the author's overall **Goal** for writing, as described in Chapter 2 of *MCAT CARS Review*. Briefly look over the Labels in your Outline to get a sense of the overall arc of the passage. Did the author follow the same train of thought throughout the passage (perhaps a description of a social policy problem and a selection of potential solutions), or did he suddenly change the focus (perhaps describing the life of an individual composer and then criticizing the classification of musical genres throughout all of music history)? Because the authors of passages used in CARS are always trying to *do* something with their text, you should always begin a Goal statement with an action word, an infinitive verb (the form of a verb starting with *to*, such as *to describe*, *to analyze*, *to rebut*, and so on). The nouns and other parts of speech that follow will fill in the subject matter and the particular focus of the author's discussion. Occasionally, an author might have multiple major Goals, in which case it's okay to use more than one verb—just be sure to use *at least* one.

In the discussion of rhetoric in Chapter 2 of *MCAT CARS Review*, we noted that the purpose of most CARS passages will fall into one of two categories: **informative** or **persuasive**. When deciding on the author's Goal, consider where he or she falls on the spectrum between taking a side and trying to remain impartial. This can help you to narrow down the appropriate purpose verb. Authors who are more informative can be said *to discuss* or *describe* a topic or, if going into greater depth, *to explain* or *analyze* it. If dealing with multiple ideas, the author might *compare* or *contrast* them. On the other hand, when authors are more persuasive, they may *support* or *advocate* a specific view, but many on the CARS section will simply *challenge*, *critique*, or *rebut* a position without offering any positive alternative. Using one or two

Real World

Creating Labels for a Passage Outline is similar to identifying the anatomy of the passage. We want to know not only what each part is but also how each part is connected and how each part relates to the greater whole.

Key Concept

The Goal of the passage is the author's purpose for writing it. In the Kaplan Method for CARS Passages, you write this Goal statement down on your scratch paper at the end of your Outline, always beginning with an infinitive verb such as *to explain*, *to argue*, or *to criticize*.

Bridge

In addition to clarifying the overall purpose of the author, the Goal statement is also useful for answering Main Idea questions, as described in Chapter 9 of *MCAT CARS Review*. The purpose verb is important too; many wrong answers in Main Idea questions will have a purpose verb with the wrong charge (*to advocate vs. to rebut*) or that is too strong or too weak (*to prove vs. to support vs. to describe*).

of the example verbs considered here will work for most CARS passages, but feel free to choose others as appropriate.

As a final note, you don't actually have to wait until completing the passage to fill in the Goal. If you are able to discover the author's purpose during your Scan, or in one of the early paragraphs, feel free to jot it down. Just be sure that when you finish the passage, you take a moment to Reflect and make sure that the Goal was in fact what you originally suspected. All things considered, the final step should take no more than about 30 seconds, and potentially quite a bit less if you managed to identify the Goal early.

4.2 Reverse-Engineering the Author's Outline

Now that you're familiar with each of the steps of the Kaplan Method for CARS Passages, you're probably still wondering what precisely you should be doing on Test Day. In this section, we discuss how to optimize your scratch paper usage, what to include in your Outline, and which portions of the passage are worth highlighting on the screen. After considering these practical concerns, you will be able to practice the method on your own until it becomes second nature for you to enter the minds of the authors of CARS passages and reconstruct their Outlines.

SCRATCH PAPER STRATEGY

During the Scan step, you can begin to construct your Outline. Each paragraph should be numbered using brief notation like *P4*. Be sure to include a spot at the end for the author's Goal; because this will always start with an infinitive verb, you can write the word *to* as a reminder. For instance, you could set up your scratch paper for a six-paragraph passage as follows:

P1.

P2.

P3.

P4.

P5.

P6.

Goal: To

This is the format that Kaplan employs in all of our example Outlines whenever we provide an explanation for a passage. Labeling becomes a matter of just filling in the blanks as you read—and the limited space will force you to be concise. Remember that abbreviation is your friend: just make sure that you're capable of understanding your own shorthand!

The challenge in constructing an effective Outline is to include the important information without writing too much. As a rule of thumb, a Label should be 5 to 7 words in a relatively simple passage and perhaps 10 to 12 words in a high-complexity passage. Labels should rarely, if ever, exceed 15 words or one line of text (keeping in mind that most students find it useful to fit two or even three columns onto their scratch paper). You may find it helpful first to construct a complete sentence in your head that captures everything discussed below and afterward just jot down a few words and symbols that will jog your memory.

WHAT TO LABEL

Once again, the four modes of reading from Chapter 3 of *MCAT CARS Review* are worth recalling. In this case, they serve as guidelines for the kind of material to include in each Label. In terms of **content**, the key ideas of each paragraph are worth jotting down, although you should stop short of trying to paraphrase every sentence. Instead, the important informational content is what is common to most if not all of the sentences in the paragraph, or the recurring theme that sets this paragraph apart from the others.

In addition to identifying the key ideas, your Outline is ultimately designed to reveal the **organization** of the passage, specifically how each paragraph functions within the larger whole. When Labeling a paragraph, think about what the paragraph is supposed to accomplish and the author's objective for placing it in the text. While many paragraphs function simply to convey information, more often than not, the content serves additional purposes, such as raising questions or problems that the author regards as significant, providing essential background for understanding an idea, supporting a claim made in the passage, or challenging a counterargument posed against the author's thesis.

The **perspectives** in the passage should be reflected in your map whenever the author has a strong opinion or in those cases when other voices speak. To Label a view as belonging to the writer of the passage, use *Author*: (or an abbreviation like *Auth*: or *Au*:) before the relevant text. Some expert test-takers may use quotes (" and ") to indicate the author's opinion; if you choose to use this strategy, avoid using quotes elsewhere in your Outline. Similarly, use colons with other proper names to indicate alternative views. An easy way to denote

MCAT Expertise

Become a two-handed test-taker! Most students use the same hand for both handwriting and using the computer mouse. Even though it may not seem like it takes long to switch between pencil and mouse, those precious seconds add up in a section with 53 questions. Thus, practice using the computer mouse with your non-writing hand. Not only will this allow you to highlight and Outline simultaneously, but you'll also find it saves you a surprising amount of time when dealing with calculations in the science sections!

positive and negative attitudes reflected in the passage is by using the shorthand of plus and minus signs. So, for instance, you could put "+++" next to an idea the author really likes. Or, if the author is ambivalent, having mixed positive and negative feelings about an issue addressed in one paragraph, you could include in your Label *(Auth ±)*. Some students prefer to use emoticons like smiley faces for the same effect.

Finally, because so many questions concern the **reasoning** of the passage, you want to pay special attention to supporting and challenging evidence as you read and be sure to identify its location in your Outline. Because many paragraphs exist simply to bolster an argument or object to one, you may already be taking into account the logic of the text when Labeling the paragraph's function. When support or challenge is not the focus of the paragraph, its presence may still be worth noting in your Outline within parentheses or after a dash.

HOW TO HIGHLIGHT

A final consideration is the use of the highlighting feature, which allows you to mark up the passage as it appears on the computer screen. Note that highlighting is never an adequate substitute for Outlining, but it becomes an extremely effective complement to the Kaplan Method for CARS Passages when used sparingly. One should *never* rely on highlighting as the primary strategy for reading a passage because highlighting will disappear if you leave a passage and return to it later. Remember that highlighting works through contrast: if you highlight most of the text, the unmarked portions would actually stand out more. Consequently, strive to adhere to the following guidelines when using this feature.

Double-Click *vs.* Click-and-Drag

On Test Day, you'll be able to highlight an entire word by double-clicking on any part of it. This always takes less time than clicking-and-dragging, so you should generally limit yourself to highlighting single words (double-clicking on two or three adjacent words is still likely quicker than clicking-and-dragging to get them all at once). If you must highlight a phrase, don't obsess about capturing it exactly: if you omit a few letters or grab an extra word or two, you'll still accomplish your intended purpose of calling attention to that specific part of the text. This sounds silly, but many test-takers will lose valuable seconds making sure to highlight precisely. Never highlight anything longer than one line of text at once.

MCAT Expertise

Do not rely on highlighting for all of the key information in a passage, but use it as a complement to your Passage Outline. Highlighting disappears if you leave a passage and come back to it later.

MCAT Expertise

Do you tend to highlight while you read on a computer? Many people will highlight online articles, emails, and other computer-based text while they read to keep their eyes moving forward. If this is true for you, get out of this habit—otherwise, the entire passage will be turned bright yellow before you move on to the questions, and any practicality of the highlighting function will be lost.

Find the First Occurrence

It's generally useful to identify when terms are introduced by an author, especially when the author provides an overt definition or offers essential background information. However, with recurring themes, it would take far too much time to highlight every instance the term appears. Scanning will often give you an idea of what these major ideas will be, but if you find a term that you didn't initially realize was important being repeated, just jump back to highlight where the term was defined before continuing with your reading.

Proper Nouns and Numbers

Names and other proper nouns, as well as dates and other numbers, have a tendency to show up in question stems as clues. Consequently, it's typically worth your time to highlight them as they appear or at least, in accordance with the preceding guideline, their first mention. You'll want to be especially careful with numbers, making sure that any answer choice that includes a time or other numerical value is consistent with the information you highlighted in the passage. The only possible "math error" you could make on the CARS section would be mixing up the numbers provided by the passage; highlighting numerical values can prevent you from committing such an easy-to-avoid mistake.

Keywords

Our final piece of advice may seem somewhat counterintuitive given the importance of keywords for reading, but as a general rule, you should not highlight most of the keywords that you encounter in a passage. While it's essential to recognize them as you read in order to appreciate the deeper levels of meaning in the text and devise a better Outline, there is little value in taking the time to highlight them. Remember that highlighting is valuable only insofar as it makes it easier to research the passage and find the information you need to answer questions correctly. When researching a question, you typically won't pay much attention to the keywords until *after* you've isolated the relevant text.

The notable exceptions to this rule are those cases in which the keywords do reveal important aspects of the passage's structure that would facilitate answering the questions. Logic keywords are the most likely to fill this role. As an alternative to marking down the location of supporting or challenging claims in your Outline, you can instead opt to Label only the conclusion on your scratch paper and just highlight the important Evidence or Refutation keywords. The other major case in which you should highlight keywords occurs with relations in longer paragraphs. If a lengthy paragraph is split by a major internal contrast or a series of steps, highlighting the Difference or Sequence keywords can illuminate the organization of the text on screen.

4.3 Practicing the Strategy

Treat the following passage as an opportunity to practice the Kaplan Method for CARS Passages. While your decision will ultimately be to do the passage *now*, you can still Scan to determine the topic and relative difficulty. Grab a sheet of scratch paper so that as you read strategically by watching out for keywords, you can Label each paragraph to create your Outline. Finally, don't forget to take a moment to Reflect and identify the author's Goal.

After attempting the method on your own with the sample passage, read the subsequent analysis section to see how closely you followed our recommended approach; then, compare your Outline with the following example Outlines. While there is not one single correct way to Outline a passage, not all Outlines are created equal: the true test of an Outline will be whether it helps you to answer the questions correctly and efficiently. However, because we won't presently be looking at any questions with this passage, you can at least use our examples as guidelines.

SAMPLE PASSAGE

Can we truly know anything with certainty? Since the dawn of the so-called "Early Modern" era in Western philosophy, this question has preoccupied both skeptics and their critics. Perhaps the most noteworthy challenger of the certainty-rejecting skeptics is René Descartes, who constructs in his seminal *Meditations* an elaborate argument that purports to ground all human knowledge on the indubitability of one's own existence. However, in his attempts, Descartes actually bolsters the case for skepticism. Indeed, later thinkers even cast doubt on the supposed surety of self-existence.

Dissatisfied with the dogmatism of his scholastic forebears, Descartes sought to clear away all the questionable but typically unquestioned "truths" handed down to him and his contemporaries, expecting that anything that remained after an onslaught of radical doubt would have to be known with certainty. Demolishing accepted opinions one by one would require volumes, so instead Descartes examines the basic categories of belief, rejecting any kind for which he can find plausible reasons for doubt.

The first *Meditation* begins the process by considering empirical knowledge, what is learned from experience by means of our senses. Descartes's most powerful argument relies upon the impossibility of discerning waking consciousness from sleeping. Who has not dreamt of "waking up" while still asleep? When I awaken, how do I know the "reality" around me is not just another layer of illusion, a dream-within-a-dream-within-a-dream? Thus, Descartes concludes that all knowledge that derives from sensation cannot be certain.

With the certainty of the *a posteriori* now eradicated, the *Meditations* turn to the *a priori*, knowledge that is independent of experience, such as mathematics and logic. This proves a more difficult task, so Descartes must introduce the possibility of a Great Deceiver, a malevolent being with godlike powers who deludes us at every turn. If I cannot prove that such an entity does not exist, then "how do I know that I am not deceived every time that I add two and three, or count the sides of a square, or judge of things yet simpler, if anything simpler can be imagined?" Readers of Orwell's *Nineteen Eighty-Four* might have an easier time of imagining this, recalling that Winston Smith under torture comes genuinely to believe that $2 + 2 = 5$.

If even arithmetic can be cast into doubt, then how could anything be known for sure? Descartes provides an answer in the second *Meditation*. Even if the Deceiver tricks me about everything else, he cannot delude me about my own existence: "Let him deceive me as much as he will, he can never cause me to be nothing so long as I think that I am something." Of course, this "I" that exists for certain does not include the physical body, which may just be an illusion, but is simply the thinking self or mind. Even so, Descartes builds on this proposition in the remainder of the *Meditations*, arguing first for the existence of a benevolent God who would not deceive us about anything perceived "clearly and distinctly," subsequently enabling him to announce an enormous ontological undertaking.

But is Descartes's foundation really so certain? Is it not possible to doubt the existence of one's own mind? In the *Genealogy of Morals*, Friedrich Nietzsche raises the possibility of an even more radical skepticism. Though Nietzsche uses the example of lightning, the same point might be clearer to English speakers with the statement "it is raining." Although "it" seems to suggest some agent independent of the action, the phrase simply means that raining is happening. Rather than saying with certainty that "I think," perhaps Descartes should have merely concluded that "thinking happens."

ANALYSIS

In conducting a Scan of the passage, a lot jumps out even in the first paragraph: the question mark in the first sentence, *Can we truly know anything with certainty?*; the quotes in *so-called "Early Modern" era in Western philosophy*; and the capitalization and italicization in *René Descartes, who constructs in his seminal* Meditations. Skimming over the first lines of the remaining paragraphs yields more references to Descartes and the *Meditations*, with a little bit of Nietzsche thrown in at the very end. This is clearly a philosophy passage, predominantly focusing on something that the thinker Descartes wrote in his book called the *Meditations*. Many students find philosophy to be the single most challenging field that appears in the CARS section, but *now* is the perfect time to see that philosophy passages are not nearly so daunting as their reputation would suggest.

Paragraph 1

When a passage opens with a question, chances are that the answer to this question will be the focus of the text. An opening question like this is not a standard rhetorical question because it does not have one uncontroversial answer that the audience could be safely assumed to adopt. It will require further work to figure out how the author would answer, and finding this answer should be our primary goal at this point. Continuing, the next sentences offer some important historical context: there are two schools of thought on the question, the *certainty-rejecting skeptics* on the one hand and their *critics* such as Descartes, who is described as *[p]erhaps the most noteworthy challenger*. This last phrase is rich in Author keywords: *noteworthy* is Positive, but the Extreme keyword *most* is canceled out by the Moderating keyword *perhaps*, so it's clear that the author's view of Descartes is not just flagrantly positive.

A critical stance toward Descartes is confirmed by the concluding sentences of the paragraph. *However* is a Difference keyword that is meant to contrast two things: Descartes's *attempts* (a Negative keyword because the suggestion is that something that is attempted could always fail) in the *Meditations* and what is *actually* (an Extreme keyword, indicating a strong author opinion) the effect, namely to *bolster* or support the opposite position—that of the skeptics. The final sentence with the mention of *supposed surety* further confirms that the author questions the soundness of Descartes's pro-certainty conclusion.

Paragraph 2

The next paragraph may seem unexpected because it lacks any kind of transitioning Relation keyword. The two sentences that constitute this paragraph both have Descartes as the subject, and the use of the past tense suggests that the author is providing historical context. The upshot is that Descartes began his quest for certainty somewhat counterintuitively: by rejecting all the suspect beliefs of his education. The key idea that untangles this paradox, however, is that *anything that remained after an onslaught of radical doubt would have to be known with certainty*. Given that *certainty* is the subject of the opening question, you'll want to note additional instances of it, such as this one.

Paragraph 3

You find a more palpable transition here, with the Sequence keywords *begins the process* signaling that more steps are to be expected. For the first step, though, you'll want to be clear on what is distinctive, and this opening sentence is useful by providing a technical term and its definition: *empirical knowledge, what is learned from experience by means of our senses*. The words that follow, *Descartes's most powerful argument relies upon* should strike you like a bolt of a lightning, containing Logic keywords as well as a strongly Positive Author keywords. What follows *relies upon* must be evidence. The two questions that follow function differently than does the opening question: they are in fact rhetorical and are supposed to support this *powerful argument*. The final sentence's *Thus, Descartes concludes* reveals a conclusion that the author seems sympathetic to but is ultimately attributed to Descartes.

Paragraph 4

Remembering the Sequence keyword from the third paragraph, we now see the next one: *turn to*. The author follows this with another technical definition: *the a priori, knowledge that is independent of experience, such as mathematics and logic*. Now, the sequence begins to emerge: first doubt experiential beliefs, then doubt mathematical ones. While the author was fond of Descartes's previous *powerful argument*, here we find *This proves a more difficult task*, a comparison that reveals the author likely regards the second argument less highly. The paragraph otherwise seems to follow the model of the preceding, with a rhetorical question, this time in quotation marks (suggesting Descartes's voice), being used for support. The reference to Orwell at the end might be baffling to you, but keep in mind that the testmakers do not expect you to know anything about a work of fiction unless it's explicitly stated in the passage, so all you need to understand is that it's being used in a supporting role.

Paragraph 5

Does the question at the start of this paragraph look familiar? It's almost like the one at the beginning, and you're told immediately about where *Descartes provides an answer*. Before reading another word, you should already recognize that this is going to be important because after the sequence of the prior two paragraphs, the author is finally returning to the point. The next sentence contains a colon followed by a quote; the colon is functioning as an equals sign, suggesting that the first statement made in the author's voice is the same as the second statement made in Descartes's. That means if you don't understand one, you can rely upon the other. The basic idea is that you can't be fooled into believing you exist when you actually don't because if you didn't exist in the first place, there would be no "you" to fool.

So how does the author feel about this? Before, we noted sympathy toward the skeptical position and even some slight hostility toward Descartes. The author's attitude is affirmed when the limits of Descartes's claims are discussed in the following sentence: that the self whose existence was supposedly proven is *simply* or merely the mind. The following *Even so* establishes a difference between what the author thinks and the text that follows: the author is suggesting that, despite this narrow limitation in the meaning of the self, Descartes still claims to ground all of knowledge on the existence of his own mind.

The end of paragraph 5 presents a rare but delightful poetic device called **alliteration** in which the author repeats the same phoneme over and over again in stressed syllables: *enabling him to announce an enormous ontological undertaking.* While this is an infrequently used device, it serves an important purpose. Much as your eye would be drawn to a bright or shiny object, your ear (or internal representation of your voice, at least) should perk up when hearing this phrase. While you should certainly not *expect* to see alliteration on Test Day, authors may use other rhetoric, poetic, or literary devices to similarly "decorate" their writing. This hints that the author particularly cares about the phrase, and it's likely to be important to the overall Goal of the passage. Note that the poetic definition of alliteration may differ from ones you've heard before—the repeated phoneme need not be located at the beginning of words but rather can occur at stressed syllables in the phrase.

Paragraph 6

Now we reach rhetorical questions once again—*really* and *not* should be dead giveaways that the author wants you to answer by saying *no, Descartes's foundation is not really so certain* and *yes, it is possible to doubt the existence of your mind*. How is this possible? Well, the author assures you that Nietzsche does it with *an even more radical skepticism* than the one that Descartes used to clear away uncertain beliefs. To be more radical, it must call into question what Descartes does not. While not revealing precisely what Nietzsche says, the author offers an analogy with familiar language used to describe the weather. If *it can rain* without *it* referring to anything that's doing the raining, then why can't the same apply to thinking? The author ends with a bit of an understatement: *perhaps Descartes should have merely concluded that "thinking happens."* The Moderating keywords suggest once again that an author of a CARS passage is hedging and making a weaker claim than is probably necessary.

Bridge

A phoneme is the smallest unit of speech sounds, like "b," "t," or "sh." Note that every major word in this alliterative phrase contains a stressed "n" sound. Phonology describes the phonemes in a given language, and it is one of the five basic components of language, as discussed in *Chapter 4 of MCAT Behavioral Sciences Review.*

Goal

Having examined each paragraph, all that remains now is to return to the big picture and Reflect on the Goal of the passage. The author is not at all neutral, attempting to persuade the audience to adopt beliefs about the validity of Descartes's arguments. The tone of the passage, moreover, is overwhelmingly critical, as reflected by all the Negative Author keywords noted above. This suggests that a purpose verb like *challenge* or *critique* would be most apt in formulating the Goal.

To be more specific, the author is challenging Descartes's answer to the question posed at the very beginning. Descartes thinks that knowledge can be known for certain and offers his reasoning in the *Meditations*, which the author recounts in several paragraphs but all for the sake of undermining it. Descartes's primary reason for believing that knowledge can be sure, according to the author, is that the existence of the thinking self cannot be doubted. But in the final paragraph, the author takes reasons from Nietzsche to suggest that it *can* in fact be doubted. You may not have realized its importance at first, but this is precisely what the author said would happen in the last sentence of the opening paragraph—*Indeed, later thinkers even cast doubt on the supposed surety of self-existence.* Authors like this one have a tendency, despite the difficulty often presented by the abstract concepts they discuss, to be straightforward about exactly what they'll do in a passage.

EXAMPLE OUTLINES

Each of the following examples is a perfectly legitimate way of Outlining the sample passage; collectively, these examples serve as varying reflections of the analysis above. If your Outline looks like any of them, or something of a hybrid, then you're off to a great start! As noted by the names provided, the major difference is in the extent of material offered. While most students will want to strive for a balance between being thorough and being concise, a bare-bones Outline has the advantage of taking the least time to construct.

The Fully Fleshed-Out Model

P1. Is certain knowledge possible? Skeptics say no; critics like Descartes say yes (Author likes skeptics)

P2. Looking for certainty, Descartes rejects any established category of belief that can be doubted

P3. D's 1st *Meditation*: beliefs from experience doubtable—supported by waking/dreaming argument

P4. More *Meditations*: beliefs independent of experience doubtable—supported by Great Deceiver idea

P5. D's 2nd *Meditation*: the thinking self is undoubtable—allows for certainty (assuming benevolent God)

P6. Author: Nietzsche undermines Descartes with reasons to doubt certainty of thinking self's existence

Goal: To explain Descartes's arguments for certain knowledge and criticize him for insufficient skepticism

The Bare-Bones Version

P1. Auth: skeptics (nothing = certain) > Descartes (self = certain)

P2. D rejects belief categories if doubtable

P3. D's argument against experience

P4. D's arg. against math/logic

P5. D's arg. for certainty of thinking self

P6. Nietzsche's criticism of ↑ (Auth +)

Goal: To challenge D's argument for certainty

A Balance of Breadth and Brevity

P1. Descartes argues for certain knowledge, grounded in self-existence (but Author prefers skepticism)

P2. D isolates certain truths by rejecting any category of doubtable belief

P3. D: can't distinguish waking/dreaming → experiential beliefs = doubtable

P4. D: Great Deceiver might fool us → math/logical beliefs = doubtable

P5. D: thinking self can't be doubted + nondeceptive God → certain knowledge

P6. Author/Nietzsche: D is wrong, thinking could happen without a self

Goal: To present and critique Descartes's argument for grounding knowledge on certain self-existence

Conclusion

With the right strategic approach, CARS passages become much more manageable. Scanning the passage to discern its difficulty can allow you to manage your time more effectively, reordering the section to work best for you. Strategic Reading means paying attention to keywords and the additional levels of meaning that they unveil. Labeling each paragraph lets you create a brief Outline, a guide for efficiently navigating the text as the questions require. Finally, Reflecting on the entire text to discern the author's Goal enhances your overall understanding as you discover how the parts function within the larger whole of the passage. The following two chapters should aid you in further developing your understanding of perhaps the most crucial aspect of CARS passages: the logic of their arguments.

CONCEPT AND STRATEGY SUMMARY

The Kaplan Method for CARS Passages

- Scan for structure
  - ○ Look for the big picture
  - ○ Assess the relative difficulty
  - ○ Decide to read *now* or *later*
- Read strategically
  - ○ Read for organization—Relation keywords
  - ○ Read for perspective—Author keywords
  - ○ Read for reasoning—Logic keywords
- Label each component
  - ○ Briefly outline the function of each paragraph
  - ○ Tag author opinions and alternative voices
  - ○ Note where to find evidence and refutations
- Reflect on your Outline
  - ○ Ask: informative or persuasive?
  - ○ Choose a purpose verb
  - ○ Record the author's Goal

Reverse-Engineering the Author's Outline

- Begin to construct your Outline before even reading the passage, numbering each paragraph and providing a space for the author's Goal.
- A good Label is brief and covers all four modes of reading (as appropriate).
  - ○ While you should find the average amount of depth that works best for you, most Labels can be written with 5 to 7 words in simple passages and 10 to 12 words in high-complexity passages.
  - ○ The key content from a paragraph should be noted in the Label.
  - ○ The Labels together form a Passage Outline, which shows the organization of the passage and how each paragraph functions within the larger whole.
  - ○ Include the author's (and others') opinions in your Outline using abbreviations or quotation marks. Positive and negative attitudes (and ambivalence) can be illustrated with plus and minus signs.
  - ○ Major aspects of logic (conclusion, evidence, and refutation) can be noted in the Label.

- Use on-screen highlighting sparingly. Remember that highlighting disappears if you leave a passage and return later.
  - Highlight the first occurrence of major terms used in the passage or where the term is defined.
  - Highlight names and proper nouns, dates, and other numbers.
  - Only highlight keywords that reveal important aspects of a passage's structure, like Logic keywords and Sequence keywords.

Practicing the Strategy

- There is no single correct way to Outline a passage, but not all Outlines are created equal.
- Your best outline is one that will help you answer the questions correctly and efficiently.

Dissecting Arguments

In This Chapter

Introduction

Imagine for a moment you wrongly believed that mitochondria were vital organs of the body, or that ligaments and tendons were what held molecules together. Even though the MCAT is ultimately a test of critical thinking, such fundamental anatomical inaccuracies would inevitably lead to misunderstood passages and missed points. The *Critical Analysis and Reasoning Skills* (CARS) section is not so different: it would be just as flawed to talk about the *truth of a concept* or the *falsity of an argument* as to describe the *kidney of a cell* or the *ribosome of an atom*. Fortunately for you, the structures employed in reasoning are *far less* complex than the intricate inner workings of human physiology, with its manifold tiers of organization and boundless cavalcade of molecular participants operating at every level. Consider this chapter your guide to the comparatively simple anatomy of arguments.

We begin the chapter with a context-setting discussion, describing three domains of discourse that are essential to distinguish when working with CARS passages. The remainder of this chapter is devoted to defining a three-tiered logical hierarchy—a simplified model of reasoning designed to give you just enough logical acumen to think clearly about CARS passages. This begins with an introduction to the lowest level, containing the elementary units of reasoning—concepts. Subsequently, we'll investigate claims, the only items that can properly be said to be true or false. At the highest tier we find arguments, which constitute the subject of our final section. Throughout the chapter, we will entertain a number of examples, but our prime specimen will be the philosophy passage from the previous chapter, ripe for dissection with its rich argumentative structure.

5.1 Domains of Discourse

When working with any academic text, as with all of the passages found in the CARS section, you will find it useful to keep distinct in your mind three levels that we call the **domains of discourse**: the natural, the textual, and the conceptual. While the language here may sound technical, the basic difference we're getting at is one that you likely already understand: things *vs.* words *vs.* ideas.

The domain of the **natural** refers to everything that can be found in the world around us. This encompasses both the objects that make up the physical world, from the simplest subatomic particles to the local galactic supercluster, and the events that occur within it, from the briefest motion of a photon to the entire lifespan of the universe. The word *natural* should be understood broadly here: it includes the distinctively "human" affairs studied by both the humanities and social sciences, like individual experiences, shared cultures, socioeconomic institutions, and historical civilizations; the "artificial" aspects of the world, such as technology and the arts; and even what might be called the "supernatural" or "metaphysical," discussed in a passage on religion, for instance.

The **textual** denotes the realm of words, sentences, and paragraphs—everything that directly faces you in an MCAT passage. It can be difficult to isolate the textual domain because language immediately points beyond itself—to objects, concepts, or perhaps both—on account of the associations that we are trained to make when learning to speak and to read. Nevertheless, it is essential to recognize that words have their own unique characteristics and structures independent of what they represent, including the rhetorical aspects of language, analyzed in Chapter 2 of *MCAT CARS Review*. Passages in literature and related disciplines tend to focus heavily on the textual domain.

Lastly, **conceptual** discourse concerns the sphere of concepts, claims, and arguments, the primary focus of this chapter and the next. Much more will be said about it below, but for now, it might be helpful to think of the conceptual domain the same way you do about some scientific phenomena. In the natural world, you will find no truly ideal gases or thermodynamic systems with 100 percent efficiency, and yet we can still talk about their distinctive properties as abstract entities. To clarify: we're not trying to suggest that there's some mystical separate world of ideas existing independently of the natural world. Rather, we're saying that there are special considerations that apply uniquely to concepts, allowing us to treat them *as though* they were their own separate sphere of existence.

POTENTIAL CONFUSIONS

It's important to stress that these domains of discourse can never be entirely separated from one another and even share a number of analogous structures, as described in Chapter 6 of *MCAT CARS Review*. Nevertheless, being able to isolate the concerns of each in your mind will help to clarify your thinking—and not only when it comes to working on the CARS section. Some of the most common errors in judgment involve the merging of one domain of discourse with another. Let's consider examples of each possibility.

Confusing the natural and textual worlds occurs when one assumes that an author's description of the world automatically corresponds to the world as it exists. It's always important to remember that every author brings her own perspective to the text, with opinions and biases that tilt the presentation of information. This is why it's generally a good idea to question what you read and think about the author's motivations behind the text. Authors are human beings who, like you, have had a limited subset of experiences but who use that finite experience to make conclusions about reality. If you can get inside an author's head and imagine where she is coming from, you'll more easily distinguish objective facts from the author's subjective impressions.

The textual and conceptual worlds are perhaps the two most often interchanged for one another, as is reflected in the common occurrence of heated disputes over the meanings of words. Have you ever had a debate with another person about an abstract issue, only to discover after several minutes of tense back-and-forth that you were actually agreeing with one another all along, just using different words to express the same ideas? (If you haven't, it may just be the case that this occurred in the past without either of you realizing it!) Conversely, just because two people use the same word does not mean that they refer to the same idea, as in the use of politically charged words such as *freedom* and *democracy*—virtually everyone today seems to agree that these are worthy ideals, yet individual conceptions of them vary dramatically.

Finally, misunderstandings between the natural and conceptual realms can be some of the most difficult to untangle. One example includes the confusion between justification and causation, which will be explained in Chapter 6 of *MCAT CARS Review*. An everyday example is the phenomenon of stereotyping, in which a person is pigeonholed into a category, then prejudicially treated as a member of a group, rather than as an individual with unique characteristics and values.

WHERE DOES LOGIC FIT?

Now that the importance of distinguishing these domains is becoming clear, you may be wondering what it has to do with the subject of these chapters: logic. Though we sometimes use the word more broadly to mean something like *structure*, in its more technical sense, **logic** is the formal study of argumentation or reasoning. This places it squarely within what we've identified as the conceptual domain.

As a branch of both mathematics and philosophy, logic is approached in a wide variety of ways, some of which are extremely advanced and well beyond the purview of the MCAT. While a complete course in formal logic might be useful for Test Day, it is certainly not essential. We deliberately employ a more simplified approach to logic that will not require an entire semester to master. The more technical aspects of our treatment will be handled in the following chapter, but the remainder of this chapter will focus on defining the key concepts in logic and how they interconnect. We stick to using terms that actually appear in CARS question stems, but note that the MCAT will not always use language quite as precisely as we do.

Within the study of logic, there are three nested levels. The most basic of these, which gives the conceptual domain its name, is the concept. Concepts relate together to make up claims, analogous to atoms making up molecules in the natural world or words making up sentences in texts. These claims, in turn, combine in arguments, like molecules forming cells or sentences composing paragraphs. At each level—concepts, claims, and arguments—there are distinct characteristics. We begin with the most basic of the elements of reasoning: concepts.

5.2 Concepts: The Basic Elements of Logic

Also known by such words as *idea* or *notion*, a **concept** is the fundamental building block of logic. Concepts have **meanings**, but they are not true or false, properly speaking. Note that the word *meaning* can be ambiguous, but here we use it specifically to point out the **connotation** or **definition** of an idea; that is, the set of distinctive properties that make the idea what it is. Concepts can still have definitions, even if they don't refer specifically to anything in the natural world: while there is no such thing as a *unicorn*, the idea still carries the sense of a magical white stallion crowned with a single golden horn.

As suggested above in the discussion of the three domains, concepts should be distinguished both from the **terms** used to represent them, on the one hand, and from the natural objects or events that might be given as **examples** of them. For instance, the concept of a *table*, as in the piece of furniture, is separate from any actual table that you may presently be sitting at and even from all the tables in the world taken together. The concept is also distinct from the combination of letters *t–a–b–l–e*, which can represent any number of other meanings, such as a noun meaning *a graphical representation of data* or a verb meaning *to delay discussion of an issue*.

The authors of passages used in CARS will often use words in ways to which you're unaccustomed, taking a term that may be familiar but using it in a narrow, specialized sense. Watch out for explicit definitions, examples, and contextual clues to help you get a sense of an idea's meaning, particularly when specific words and phrases are frequently repeated. Be warned, though, that many authors will use multiple terms interchangeably to refer to the same underlying concept and that, even further, questions in CARS can employ synonyms and paraphrases of ideas in different wording than is used in the passage. In short, it will be essential on Test Day to look for concept-for-concept correspondences, not exact word-for-word matches.

MCAT Expertise

MCAT students often lose points because they search for answer choices that use exactly the same wording as the passage. It is not uncommon for the testmakers to write answer choices that reflect the same concept using different words (a different textual representation).

RELATIONS OF IDEAS

In Chapter 3 of *MCAT CARS Review*, Relation keywords were introduced as a tool for recognizing the organization within texts. Many Relation keywords are useful on a textual level, revealing how the author intends diverse sentences to be connected. However, in addition to revealing points of continuity or contrast within a text, Relation keywords will also tie ideas together in distinctive ways. In our description of Relation keywords, we pointed out that the most basic relationships are Similarity and Difference, but much greater specificity is possible, such as Opposition, Sequence, and Comparison. One other important relation to note is that between a whole and its parts—so, for instance, the *golden horn* is a concept that is also a part of the concept *unicorn*, which constitutes a larger whole.

In addition to relating to each other, concepts can also relate to parts of the other domains of discourse. On the one hand, a natural object or event might *exemplify* or *embody* a concept, meaning that the entity serves as an example of it. On the other hand, a term or word might *represent*, *designate*, or *refer to* a concept, meaning that the word or phrase is being used to stand in place for the concept. While these are not technically relations between ideas, you should still be aware of these interactions between the different realms of discourse because these words are used this way in CARS questions.

5.3 Claims: The Bearers of Truth Value

What distinguishes a **claim** (also called an *assertion*, *statement*, *proposition*, *belief*, or *contention*) from a mere concept is **truth value**, the capacity to be either true or false. While claims may be quite complex (potentially consisting of numerous concepts related together in diverse ways), having a truth value requires only two parts at minimum: a **subject** and a **predicate**, like the most important nouns and verbs in a sentence. Thus, *the Abominable Snowman* is not a claim but rather a subject without a predicate, making it a concept with meaning but no truth value. However, *the Abominable Snowman is eight feet tall*, *everybody loves the Abominable Snowman*, and even *the Abominable Snowman doesn't exist* are all claims because all are either true or false, in addition to being meaningful.

Just as it's essential to know the difference between a term and the concept that it denotes, so too should you be able to distinguish between the sentences of a text and the *claims* that underlie them. Again, authors often find many ways of making the same point, echoing a claim while varying the language that they use to sound less repetitive. Furthermore, CARS question stems and answer choices will contain their own clauses, which could depart dramatically from the words the author uses while still retaining the same sense. This is all the more reason for distinguishing between the textual (the words the author uses) and the conceptual (the ideas those words represent).

CONSISTENCY AND CONFLICT

Claims are important in CARS on account of the relationships that they share with one another, particularly those that concern truth value. These must be distinguished from the relationships mentioned above that concepts share, which are based on meaning, not truth. **Consistency** is the simplest relation between claims: if two or more statements can be true simultaneously, they are described with language like *consistent*, *compatible*, or *in agreement*. Bear in mind that this is a pretty minimal relationship. Most logically consistent claims have absolutely nothing to do with one another: *Though commonly perceived as overwhelmingly motivated by the struggle to end slavery, the American Civil War was in actuality the product of a hodgepodge of disparate political, economic, and cultural forces, among which abolitionism was but one prominent factor* is completely consistent with *I like cookies.*

Because being in agreement is "easy," the opposite relation is fairly extreme: when CARS passages and questions use terms like *inconsistent*, *contradictory*, or *conflicting*, they refer to a set of claims (typically just two) for which it is *impossible* that all be simultaneously true. Contradictory claims could be outright negations of one another, differing only in that one includes a word like *not* or a prefix like *un–*, or they could be incompatible in a more subtle way like *it is sunny* and *there is a thunderstorm outside.*

Key Concept

Claims are the middlemen in the logical hierarchy, composed themselves of concepts and their relationships and, in turn, composing arguments. Claims consist of at least a subject and a predicate, and they have both meaning and truth value (the capacity to be true or false).

Bridge

Note that sometimes the MCAT will use consistency terms in conjunction with *most* or *least,* asking for the *claim that is most conflicting* or one that is *least consistent with the author's ideas.* In those cases when agreement is treated as a matter of degree, the terms are being used with meanings closer to *similar* and *dissimilar.* See the discussion of analogical reasoning in Chapter 6 of *MCAT CARS Review* for more on this topic.

SUPPORT

Because it is a factor in about half of all questions you'll encounter in CARS, there is no relationship more important to understand than **support**. This is a special type of connection that is unidirectional in nature, unlike the "two-way street" of consistency that treats claims as equal in status. A statement is *supporting* when its truth would increase the likelihood that the claim *supported* by it is also true. Thus, for one claim to support another, the two must also be consistent. At the same time, unless the argument is circular, support will not flow the other way.

An illustration of this latter point can be seen when considering the philosophy passage from Chapter 4 of *MCAT CARS Review*, when the author notes in the third paragraph that *Descartes concludes that all knowledge that derives from sensation cannot be certain* because of the *impossibility of discerning waking consciousness from sleeping*. In effect, the claim *dreaming cannot be distinguished from waking reality* supports the statement *empirical knowledge is uncertain*. If we were to ask why we should believe that waking can't be distinguished from sleeping, Descartes could not reasonably say *because empirical knowledge is uncertain* because that's what he was originally trying to convince us of in the first place!

The opposite of support is the relationship sometimes known as a *refutation*, *challenge*, or *objection*. This will be addressed below in the discussion of counterarguments.

> **Key Concept**
>
> Support is a unidirectional relationship between claims. If one claim supports another, the truth of the first would make the truth of the second more likely, but *not* vice-versa

5.4 Arguments: Conclusions and Evidence

In support relationships, claims get special names. A mere contention becomes a supported **conclusion** as long as it's accompanied by supporting **evidence.** Evidence is like the friend who vouches for you to get into the VIP area at a nightclub (*Conclusions only!*): it offers reason to "trust" that the conclusion is what it claims to be. In other words, evidence is an answer to the question *Why should I believe that?* Together, the evidence, the conclusion, and the one-way connection between them (support) constitute the simplest form of an **argument**. This is what the example of support from the Descartes passage looks like in argumentative form:

- **Evidence**: It is impossible to tell the difference between dreaming and being awake.
- **Conclusion**: Knowledge gained from sense experience is inherently uncertain.

While one piece of evidence is sufficient to make a claim count as a conclusion, authors typically rely upon multiple sources of support, sometimes even providing additional reasons for believing the evidence provided. So, continuing with Descartes,

> **Key Concept**
>
> An argument is the combination of one claim, known as the conclusion, and one or more other assertions, known as the evidence, explicitly used to support it.

you might ask why you should believe the supposed evidence is actually true, that dreaming is truly indistinguishable from waking life. The author never says directly what Descartes's reasoning is but instead uses a rhetorical question *Who has not dreamt of "waking up" while still asleep?* to suggest a common human experience. If we made this into an argument, now we would have the following:

- **Evidence**: You have at least once in your life had a dream in which you thought you woke up, only to discover later that you had still been dreaming.
- **Conclusion**: It is impossible to tell the difference between dreaming and being awake.

This may seem peculiar because what was before called the evidence is now the conclusion. Can the exact same statement be both evidence and conclusion? Yes, but only in relation to two different claims. This is nothing special: the same man can be both a son and a father, the same woman both a daughter and a mother. Anytime a claim is used to *support* something else, it's acting as evidence; but whenever it in turn *is supported by* something else, it's acting as a conclusion. If we treated the second argument as a "subargument" within the first, we could represent it like this:

- **Subevidence**: You have at least once in your life had a dream in which you thought you woke up, only to discover later that you had still been dreaming.
- **Subconclusion/evidence**: It is impossible to tell the difference between dreaming and being awake.
- **Conclusion**: Knowledge gained from sense experience is inherently uncertain.

Or, as we'll see more extensively in Chapter 6 of *MCAT CARS Review*, we can use arrows to represent the relevant support relationships, simplifying the depiction of the argument further:

You have at least once in your life had a dream in which you thought you woke up, only to discover later that you had still been dreaming.

It is impossible to tell the difference between dreaming and being awake.

Knowledge gained from sense experience is inherently uncertain.

When determining relationships such as these, you can use the textual clues discussed in Chapter 3 of *MCAT CARS Review*, especially Evidence and Conclusion

MCAT Expertise

When authors employ especially difficult arguments, you may find it useful to sketch a diagram on your scratch paper next to your Outline, using arrows to denote the support connections. Place the author's main conclusion, or thesis, either at the top with arrows pointing up toward it, or, as we model in the text, at the bottom with down arrows. Multiple pieces of evidence for the same conclusion would appear as branches extending from a common stem; thus, we sometimes call these drawings "argument trees."

keywords (two of the subtypes of Logic keywords). However, as noted there, these keywords are less common than the other two types, and some authors use them quite sparingly. Be alert for hidden support relationships!

COUNTERARGUMENTS

An additional complication to this picture is the **counterargument**, or an argument made against (counter to) a particular conclusion. Counterarguments are also known as refutations, objections, or challenges, and they can be indicated through the use of the aptly named Refutation keywords from Chapter 3 of *MCAT CARS Review*. While some writers will *only* offer counterarguments, their purpose being to argue against some claim, many authors raise counterarguments merely for the sake of refuting them, which is an indirect way to support their conclusion.

The passage from the last chapter provides a key example of this. The author is ultimately interested in arguing in favor of the skeptical position, which can be summarized by the claim *certain knowledge is impossible*. Arguing in favor of a negative is difficult, so the author opts instead to argue *against* Descartes, who tries to support the exact opposite position, that *certain knowledge is possible*. Thus, the author begins the fifth paragraph (playing off of a conclusion supported in the previous paragraph) asking, *If even arithmetic can be cast into doubt, then how could anything be known for sure?* The author would just as soon answer this question by saying that nothing *can* be known for sure, but instead gives us Descartes's opposing view. Up to this point, we could summarize the counterargument like so, this time putting the conclusion first:

- **Conclusion**: Certain knowledge is impossible.
- **Refutation**: As long as I think that I am something, I must exist.

If I can be certain that I exist, then certain knowledge *would* be possible, which is *inconsistent* with the conclusion. However, the author is not content to let Descartes win—and yes, for many authors of passages used in CARS, it is effectively about who wins or loses the argument. In the final paragraph, the author responds to the refutation, challenging Descartes's counterargument, thereby supporting the original conclusion. That looks something like this:

- **Conclusion**: Certain knowledge is impossible.
- **Refutation**: As long as I think that I am something, I must exist.
- **Counter-refutation**: Just because there is thinking does not mean there is an "I" who thinks.

Again, keep in mind that refutations will not show up in every CARS passage and that arguments only minimally require two claims: one conclusion and one statement of evidence.

Key Concept

Unstated claims in arguments are known as inferences. Inferences are either assumptions (unstated evidence) or implications (unstated conclusions).

INFERENCES

While an argument could contain as little as one stated conclusion and one piece of stated evidence, most arguments contain hidden or implicit parts as well. The most commonly appearing terms for these are *inferences*, *assumptions*, and *implications*. As verbs, *imply* designates the action of a writer hinting at something without saying it outright, while *infer* indicates the reader's role in deciphering the hints. Whether the unstated conclusion that is reached is called an inference or an implication is simply a difference in emphasis, not meaning. That said, for the sake of precision, whenever we use the word **implication**, we specifically will refer to an unstated conclusion, and **assumption** will be used only for unstated evidence. **Inference** will be used generally to cover any unstated part of an argument, whether an implication or an assumption.

It's important to note that assumptions and implications are not simply claims that are *possibly* or *probably* true given what is said. Rather, inferences must be true or—at the very least—must be highly probable, the most likely option among the alternatives. One way to recognize an inference is by the negative effect it would have on the argument if it were denied. This is a procedure that is employed in the strategy we call the Denial Test, explained in Chapter 10 of *MCAT CARS Review* in the strategy discussion for the appropriately named Inference questions.

In the passage from before, the author actually unearths an assumption in Descartes's argument for the certainty of self-existence in the fifth paragraph by pointing out that *this "I" that exists for certain does not include the physical body, which may just be an illusion, but is simply the thinking self or mind*. We could summarize it as follows:

- **Conclusion**: As long as I think I am something, I must exist.
- **Assumption**: "I" only refers to the mind that thinks, and does not include the body.

If this assumption were denied, it would mean that the existence of the physical body could be certain. But can we actually be certain about the existence of our bodies? Descartes himself gives us reason not to think so because he argues earlier that waking and dreaming cannot be distinguished, meaning that I could just be dreaming that I have a body when I'm actually just some brain floating about in a dark laboratory vat. Thus, because Descartes suggests the existence of the body is uncertain, but argues that the existence of the self ("I") is certain, then it must be the case that his concept of the self excludes the body—and this is the assumption that the author identifies.

STRENGTHENING AND WEAKENING

Recall that only claims have truth value; it is a misstatement to say that an argument is true or false. Rather than a simple either/or, the **validity** or **strength** of arguments varies along a continuum with certain proof at one end, complete refutation at the other, and most arguments (virtually all of the ones you see on the MCAT) falling somewhere short of either extreme, with evidence making conclusions more probable and refutations making them less probable.

Questions, particularly both types of Strengthen–Weaken questions (discussed in Chapters 10 and 11 of *MCAT CARS Review*) will often not take the force of a given argument for granted, requiring you instead to imagine how it might be modified. A higher quantity or quality of supporting evidence will *strengthen*, *bolster*, or *further* an argument. This evidence can come in many forms; different fields of study can diverge widely in the types of support that practitioners of the discipline find compelling. For instance, quotations from a novel carry a lot of weight in a literary discussion advocating for an interpretation of that specific piece of fiction, but they would be of much more questionable worth if offered in support of historical claims about events that occurred during its writing.

On the other hand, a claim is said to *weaken*, *challenge*, or *undermine* an argument whenever its truth would make the conclusion more likely to be false. Using the language just introduced, such claims serve as refutations or counterarguments. Note that most refutations do not come in the form of outright contradictions of the original conclusion or evidence. In other words, while inconsistencies will definitely weaken an argument, there are many other ways to pose challenges than simply asserting the opposite. So if an author is, say, making general claims about US citizens on the basis of results from a psychological survey, his argument would be undermined by evidence that the sample used was demographically unrepresentative.

There are only a few basic ways to strengthen or weaken an argument. To see these, it helps to return to the concept of a *table*, using it now as an analogy, with the tabletop substituting for the conclusion and each piece of support represented by a leg of the table. Now, a table might be supported with one sturdy central leg, with two equally balanced legs at either end, or with any number of smaller legs that distribute its weight evenly among them. Regardless of how many legs the table actually has, there are really only three ways to strengthen it (to enhance the support of the tabletop): to add a new leg, reinforce an existing leg, or remove a heavy weight that threatens to bring the table crashing down. Similarly, an argument can be supported by bringing in an entirely new piece of evidence, by providing additional support for an existing piece of evidence, or by challenging a counterargument to its conclusion.

Key Concept

Arguments are evaluated on the basis of their strength or validity, which varies along a spectrum. An argument is strengthened whenever the truth of its conclusion is made more probable and weakened whenever it is made less probable.

In terms of weakening, the same analogy comes to bear. A tabletop will come crashing to the ground if a heavy enough weight is added, just as an argument will collapse if a new refutation is sufficiently weighty. Supporting a refutation that was raised in the passage (which could be a matter of undermining the author's response to that refutation) is just like piling on additional weight. The third and final option for weakening is to knock the legs out from under the table, typically by attacking one that is crucially placed. Analogously, challenging a key piece of evidence can be just as effective at weakening an argument as challenging the conclusion directly.

Conclusion

While academic texts can be vague and subject to interpretation, every question you face on the CARS section will have only one defensible answer. The value of logic is precisely in its ability to clarify your thinking, allowing you to mirror the cognitive processes the testmakers use, and home in on correct responses. As noted in Chapter 1 of *MCAT CARS Review*, of all CARS questions, 30 percent involve *Reasoning Within the Text* and 40 percent require *Reasoning Beyond the Text*. Because even *Foundation of Comprehension* questions can involve making inferences, you can expect more than three-quarters of your points on CARS to benefit from clear logical thinking. To develop your capacity for this even further, we explore two additional applications of logic in the following chapter.

CONCEPT AND STRATEGY SUMMARY

Domains of Discourse

- The **natural domain** corresponds to objects, events, and experiences—everything that can be found in the world around us.

- The **textual domain** corresponds to words, sentences, and paragraphs—everything that directly faces you in an MCAT passage.

- The **conceptual domain** corresponds to concepts, claims, and arguments—everything that underlies logic.

Concepts: The Basic Elements of Logic

- **Concepts** are ideas that have meanings (definitions or connotations).

- Ideas can be related through various relations, which are often indicated with Relation keywords in a passage.

  - Similarity and Difference are very common Relation keywords.

  - Opposition, Sequence, and Comparison keywords are less common, but they are significant when they occur in a passage.

  - The relation between the whole and its parts can be important in some CARS passages.

Claims: The Bearers of Truth Value

- **Claims** can also be called assertions, statements, propositions, beliefs, or contentions.

- Claims are made up of combinations of concepts and relationships of ideas.

- They possess truth value and can thus be true or false.

- Claims can also be related through various relationships.

  - If two claims are **consistent** (compatible or in agreement) with one another, then both can be true simultaneously.

  - If two claims are **inconsistent** (contradictory or conflicting) with one another, then it is impossible for both to be true simultaneously.

  - If one claim **supports** another, then this claim being true would make the other claim more likely to be true as well.

  - If one claim **challenges** (refutes or objects to) another, then this claim being true would make the other claim more likely to be false.

Arguments: Conclusions and Evidence

- At a minimum, arguments contain three parts: a **conclusion**, its **evidence**, and the one-way path of **support** between them.

- **Counterarguments**, also called **refutations**, **objections**, or **challenges**, are the opposite of evidence because they go against the conclusion.

- **Inferences** are unstated parts of arguments.

  ○ **Assumptions** are unstated pieces of evidence.

  ○ **Implications** are unstated conclusions.

  ○ Inferences are claims that must be true or—at the very least—must be highly probable.

- There are three main ways of strengthening an argument:

  ○ One could provide a new piece of evidence that supports the conclusion.

  ○ One could support evidence that already exists to support the conclusion.

  ○ One could challenge refutations against the conclusion.

- There are three main ways of weakening an argument:

  ○ One could provide a new refutation that goes against the conclusion.

  ○ One could support refutations that already exist.

  ○ One could challenge evidence for the conclusion.

Formal Logic

In This Chapter

Introduction

If you think you now know everything that is important to know about logic, then you're in store for a surprise in this chapter. Claims such as the one in the preceding sentence are known as conditionals, and they play a major role in logic. Our present discussion builds on the logical foundations laid in Chapter 5 of *MCAT CARS Review*. We will use the definitions presented in that chapter as a launching point to explore some more formalized aspects of logic. These are the most abstract topics considered in the entire book, so it's essential to be well versed in the established terminology and to proceed slowly and methodically so that the material will not be made even more difficult than it intrinsically is.

Now that you understand the basic anatomy of arguments, we can investigate two special forms of argumentation commonly employed in CARS passages and asked about in questions. The first of these, arguments made using conditional claims, is the more fundamental of the two, with conditional relationships featured in some form in every passage and playing some role in most CARS questions. Consequently, the first part of our discussion explains conditional arguments' basic structure and operation, while the next part examines how conditionals manifest themselves in CARS passages and questions, especially in the commonly appearing relationships of justification and causation. The final part of the chapter is devoted to the other major form of argument, analogical reasoning, employed by many passage authors and tested in almost every question type in the category the AAMC calls *Reasoning Beyond the Text*.

Bridge

Your understanding of this chapter is contingent on having internalized the terminology defined in Chapter 5 of *MCAT CARS Review*. Make sure you know the difference between the natural, textual, and conceptual domains and make sure you can discriminate between a concept, a claim, and an argument.

6.1 The Logic of Conditionals

The term **conditional** ultimately refers to not just one but an entire class of uni-directional relationships between two items. These items could be from any of the domains discussed in the previous chapter (the natural, textual, or logical), but we'll use a word from the textual domain, **terms**, to discuss the items generically. Different kinds of conditionals will be discussed in the second part of the chapter, but all of them have the same basic form and logical characteristics.

REPRESENTING CONDITIONALS

Assuming that **X** and **Y** are two terms, and that the arrow (→) indicates the direction of the connection, the following formulation expresses the conditional relationship:

$$X \rightarrow Y$$

Consider this a representation of the basic concept of the conditional. But what does this really mean? What exactly is the connection signified by the arrow? Let's assume for a moment that the terms **X** and **Y** denote claims, which (as detailed in Chapter 5 of *MCAT CARS Review*) are evaluated on the basis of their truth value—the potential to be either true or false (but not both at the same time). When working with claims, we could rewrite the conditional relationship in this slightly less formal way:

If **X** is true, then **Y** is true.

Note that while it is made up of a relationship between two claims, this is itself a kind of statement with its own truth value. We'll call this a **conditional claim**; that is, it is a statement that has a meaning that could be captured equivalently by using an **if–then** assertion, as above. Moreover, adopting the common convention, we'll designate the *if* term the **antecedent** and the *then* term the **consequent**. Here's a concrete example, with the antecedent and consequent in bold:

If it's true that **you are in Pennsylvania**, then it's also true that **you are in the United States of America**.

Or more simply:

If **you're in Pennsylvania**, then **you're in the United States.**

What is distinctive about such claims is that their truth, formally speaking, depends on only the truth of the antecedent and consequent. As long as it's impossible for **X** to be true the same time that **Y** is false (that you could be in Pennsylvania without being in the United States), then the conditional statement is true. In other words, the **conditional relationship** can be defined as the impossibility of having a true antecedent and a false consequent.

This can be represented formally in what is known as a **truth table**. In Table 6.1, all four possible combinations of the truth of **X** and **Y** are presented, as well as the resultant truth of the conditional claim in the final column:

X	Y	$X \rightarrow Y$
true	true	**true**
true	false	**false**
false	true	**true**
false	false	**true**

Table 6.1. Truth Table for Conditional Claims

Returning to the location example, we know that it's simply not possible for the antecedent (*you're in Pennsylvania*) to be true while the consequent (*you're in the United States*) is false. This is because Pennsylvania is completely contained within the United States. Thus, we can say with confidence that the statement *If you're in Pennsylvania, then you're in the United States of America* is true.

Notice that this does not work the other way around; a conditional is unidirectional. You say something entirely different, something that is factually false, when you claim, *If you are in the United States, then you are in Pennsylvania*. In addition to the other 49 states, the District of Columbia, and 16 territories including Puerto Rico, Guam, and American Samoa, the United States occupies many military bases and diplomatic embassies, effectively spanning the globe. As can be seen, there are many ways to be in the United States without being in Pennsylvania.

Now here is a crucial point that cannot be stressed enough: *a conditional claim can still be true even if you know the antecedent is itself false*. In our geographical example, it doesn't matter whether you're in Maryland (in which case **X** is false but **Y** is true) or in New Zealand (for which both **X** and **Y** would be false). Neither of those is what might be thought of as the forbidden combination: a true antecedent plus a false consequent. No matter how hard you try, there's simply no way to be in Pennsylvania without also being in the United States (that's true even for the foreign embassies and consulates located in Philadelphia, which would count as being on neither US nor Pennsylvania soil, from the standpoint of international law).

NECESSARY *vs.* SUFFICIENT CONDITIONS

Besides using the language of *antecedent* and *consequent*, there is another noteworthy way of understanding the relationship embodied in a conditional that divides the relationship in two by considering it from the perspective of each term. In this alternative account, each of the two terms in $X \rightarrow Y$ counts as a type of condition. Thus, **X** would be the **sufficient condition**, while **Y** would be the **necessary condition**.

Key Concept

Another way of conceptualizing a conditional is to think of it as two simultaneous relationships. In the conditional claim *if X, then Y*, X is a sufficient condition of Y, while Y is a necessary condition of X.

MCAT Expertise

In more complex cases, you'll find that there can be more than one necessary condition or more than one sufficient condition. Suppose that both **X** and **Y** together lead to **Z**. We would then say that **X** and **Y** are *mutually necessary and jointly sufficient* for **Z**. For instance, to be a mother it is not simply sufficient to be female, but one also needs to be a parent. Thus, being female (**X**) and being a parent (**Y**) are mutually necessary and jointly sufficient for being a mother (**Z**). Though rare, this complication has appeared in past MCAT exams, including once in an extremely challenging question on linguistics that required understanding the two notions, only briefly explained in the accompanying passage.

Key Concept

The contrapositive is a statement with a different connotation (emphasizing the necessary condition, rather than the sufficient) but that is logically equivalent to a conditional assertion. For instance, the contrapositive of *if X is true, then Y is true* can be written as either *if Y is not true, then X is not true* or *if Y is false, then X is false*.

Or, to state it in a way that highlights the relation between the two terms, in $X \rightarrow Y$, X is a sufficient condition of Y, while Y is a necessary condition of X. Let's consider each side of this, in turn.

Saying that **X** is **sufficient** for **Y** is equivalent to saying that it's impossible to have **X** without also having **Y**. So, to return to our intuitive geographical example, it's enough to know that you're in Pennsylvania—it doesn't matter whether it's Pittsburgh, Philadelphia, or Punxsutawney—to be able to conclude that you're in the United States. In short, being in Pennsylvania is *sufficient* for being in the United States. This is really just another way of expressing the conditional relationship as the impossibility of a true antecedent and a false consequent.

While the relationship of sufficiency is the aspect of the conditional that we're already familiar with, necessity is a bit new, although it's simply the same relationship considered from the opposite perspective. Saying that **Y** is **necessary** for **X** is like saying that **Y** is a **prerequisite** or **requirement** of **X**. This amounts to a negative claim: if **Y** is not true, then **X** is not true. If we consider the example from before from this perspective, it becomes:

If you are **not in the United States**, then you are **not in Pennsylvania**.

This statement is logically equivalent to *If you are in Pennsylvania, then you are in the United States*. However, even though the two versions of the claim will always have the same truth value, their meanings are not identical—if nothing else, there is a difference in point of reference. This alternative form, which emphasizes a necessary condition, is even known by a special name, the contrapositive.

FORMING THE CONTRAPOSITIVE

Whenever an author makes any kind of conditional claim, it is always possible to translate the conditional claim into other relationships. Most notably, one can form the logically equivalent assertion known as the contrapositive. By definition, the **contrapositive** of *if X, then Y* is *if not Y, then not X*. Alternatively, this can be represented using a tilde (~) to stand for negation (~X thus means *not X* or *the negation of X*):

Conditional: $X \rightarrow Y$

Contrapositive: $\sim Y \rightarrow \sim X$

One of the most useful reasons for forming the contrapositive is that it's a guaranteed inference, a logical equivalent for any conditional claim made in a passage. Whenever you recognize Logic keywords or one of the English translations of a conditional claim (listed in Table 6.2 below), you'll want to keep in mind that a rendition of its contrapositive could appear as a correct answer.

6.2 Applications of Conditionals

Now that you've seen how conditionals work as logical structures, let's consider how they function in CARS passages and questions. Remember that with each of the following cases, although the logical form of the relationship is identical, the actual relationships are not equivalent because they operate within the different domains of discourse described in Chapter 5 of *MCAT CARS Review*.

ONE FORM, MANY FUNCTIONS

Although we have been considering only claims as the antecedent and consequent terms in a conditional, these terms could take some other form, as noted earlier. For example, the consequent could be a concept that is an essential part of the definition of a larger concept, which would be the antecedent. This would be an example of a whole–parts relationship, which you can now see can be represented as a conditional in which the *whole* being defined is an antecedent or sufficient condition and any defining *part* is a consequent or necessary condition.

For instance, consider the relationship between the concept *unicorn* and the concept *horn*, from an example first posed in the previous chapter: unicorn → horn. The first idea is a sufficient condition for the second: if you know you're dealing with a unicorn, then you know you're dealing with a concept that includes a horn in its definition. Simultaneously, the consequent is a necessary condition of the antecedent (forming the contrapositive): no horn entails no unicorn. Like any conditional, this doesn't work the other way around: a horn doesn't guarantee a unicorn because the concept of a narwhal, a rhinoceros, or even certain lizards would also include a horn in its definition.

Other instances of conditionals will fall under the natural domain of discourse rather than the conceptual. For example, an object and its essential components or characteristics (more whole–parts relationships) could be represented as conditionals: *object → components* or *object → characteristic*. A case of the first is the connection between a living human body and an intact brainstem—though other parts may be present, no human can live independently without a functioning brainstem. The latter can be seen in the relationship between plant cells and cell walls. While other organisms can also have cell walls (fungi, for example, have a cell wall composed of *chitin*), all known plant cells possess a cell wall. Thus, being a plant cell is sufficient for having the characteristic of a cell wall.

These are but a few of the possible forms that a conditional relationship could take. Yet while there are many specific iterations, two in particular stand out as being by far the most common. Moreover, as originally suggested in Chapter 3 of *MCAT*

CARS Review, these two relationships are the ones most commonly revealed with the use of Logic keywords.

JUSTIFICATION *vs.* CAUSATION

The term **justification** is ultimately another way of talking about the relationship of logical support. In this particular relationship, the two items in the conditional are claims, aspects of the conceptual domain of discourse: the antecedent is the **evidence**, and the consequent is the **conclusion**. In fact, any argument can be made into a single conditional relationship if all the evidence is lumped together into one single statement with a lot of conjunctions (*and*s).

While justification is a kind of conceptual conditional, connecting two claims, **causation** is another natural connection, one that links two *events*. Unlike a mere **correlation**, in which two occurrences are found to accompany one another, causation is a one-way relationship, like any conditional. In this instance, however, the order is temporal: the antecedent (cause) must occur before the consequent (effect). Moreover, in contrast to sequences of events that may happen coincidentally, causes are directly responsible for leading to their effects. Proving this last characteristic of causality can be particularly challenging, so robustly supporting a causal assertion is no easy task.

Both causation and justification are conditional relationships, but they are quite distinct. On the one hand, causes and effects are *events* in the *natural* world, with the cause always preceding the effect in time. On the other hand, pieces of evidence and conclusions are *claims* about the world, part of the conceptual domain of discourse, with a relationship that might not follow the arrow of time. This is evident in the following contrast:

The dinosaurs were turned into fossils **because of** an asteroid's catastrophic impact.

vs.

We know that there was a catastrophic asteroid impact **because of** evidence provided by dinosaur fossils.

The second argument is distinct insofar as it does not address the dinosaurs and the asteroid directly, as the first one does, but rather concerns our *knowledge* of the asteroid and the *evidence* that the fossils provide. While the asteroid may be (at least indirectly) the *cause* of the fossils, without a time machine we have access only to what remains of the fossils in the present day. Because we are able to see only the *effect*, we have to make an inference to figure out the cause.

Bridge

Hill's criteria can be used to support the likelihood of causality in a relationship. While only temporality is absolutely necessary for causation, it is not sufficient. The other criteria include strength, dose–response relationship, consistency, plausibility, consideration of alternate explanations, experimentation, specificity, and coherence. Hill's criteria are discussed in Chapter 11 of *MCAT Physics and Math Review*.

The upshot of this is that whenever you encounter Evidence or Conclusion keywords, you should always clarify the domain of discourse in which the author is writing. If the terms in the conditional are natural, then *because* indicates a cause, and *consequently* denotes an effect. When the terms are conceptual entities instead (specifically claims with truth value), words like *since* point to evidence, while *therefore* and *thus* designate conclusions. Your default assumption should be justification because this relationship tends to be more commonly tested.

LOGICAL TRANSLATIONS

While as a general rule, an Evidence keyword precedes an antecedent or sufficient condition and a Conclusion keyword precedes a consequent or necessary condition, there are some ways of expressing a conditional relationship that are less clear about distinguishing the two terms. To aid you in recognizing some of these more elaborate articulations, note that each of the terms in Table 6.2 is logically equivalent to the basic conditional statement $X \rightarrow Y$ (*If I'm in Pennsylvania, then I'm in the United States*).

If **X**, then **Y**.	If I'm in Pennsylvania, then I'm in the United States.
X is sufficient for **Y**.	Being in Pennsylvania is sufficient for being in the United States.
All **X** are **Y**.	All those in Pennsylvania are in the United States.
X only if **Y**.	I'm in Pennsylvania only if I'm in the United States.
If not **Y**, then not **X**. [*Contrapositive*]	If I'm not in the United States, then I'm not in Pennsylvania.
Y is necessary for **X**.	Being in the United States is necessary for being in Pennsylvania.
Only **Y** are **X**.	Only those in the United States are in Pennsylvania.
Not **X** unless **Y**.	I'm not in Pennsylvania unless I'm in the United States.

Table 6.2. English Translations of X → Y

6.3 Analogical Reasoning

The final formal application of logic worth studying for Test Day is associated almost exclusively with one category of questions. That said, as you'll see in Chapter 11 of *MCAT CARS Review*, the *Reasoning Beyond the Text* category constitutes two-fifths of all CARS questions. These are relatively easy to identify because they always involve new information (in the question stem, the set of answer choices, or both) that is not stated or even suggested by the passage and that may not even seem to be related at first. In one typical pattern, words like *Suppose*, *Assume*, and *Imagine* precede an elaborate scenario that fills several lines of text, followed up by a question that connects this new content to the author or passage. Making the appropriate connections to address such questions requires a skill that may seem so obvious that it defies explanation: recognizing similarities.

SIMILARITY, REVISITED

In Chapter 3 of *MCAT CARS Review*, we noted how Similarity keywords reveal continuities within texts, often cluing you into repetitions or ancillary details. These tend to be less significant than contrasts and other more complex relationships, signaled by the other Relation keywords. Nevertheless, similarity as a concept is actually far more important than this strategic guideline would initially suggest.

Similarity is one of those ideas that seem obvious until you try to explain them. At its most extreme, similarity becomes *identity*, as would be the case when two terms are used to reference one single natural entity: the so-called *Morning Star* and *Evening Star* are identical because both terms refer to the planet Venus. Slightly less extreme cases of similarity would be exact duplicates, such as photocopies of documents, backups of computer files, the genetics of monozygotic twins, coins of the same denomination, or interchangeable machine parts.

With CARS passages and questions, similarity is typically more than a simple matter of two terms that refer to the same thing or duplicates. Most concepts that you'll be comparing will be complex, with many characteristics, some of which will overlap and some of which will not. This complexity depends upon the relationship between a whole and its parts, introduced in the preceding chapter and noted earlier as a form of conditional. These more involved comparisons, known as **analogies**, have special considerations governing their use in arguments.

ARGUMENTS FROM ANALOGY

An **argument from analogy** begins on the basis of similarities between two things to argue for an additional commonality between them. In other words, it concludes that something (typically an *object* or *event* in the natural domain, though potentially a complex *concept* instead) has a certain quality because it is like something else with a similar characteristic. Analogies always contain two terms: the **known** entity is the one with characteristics that are already well established, while the **unknown** entity is only partially understood. If we call the known **K** and the unknown **U**, we arrive at the following formalization of an argument from analogy:

- **Evidence**: **K** and **U** share similar corresponding characteristics (K_1 and U_1, K_2 and U_2, K_3 and U_3, and so on).
- **Evidence**: **K** possesses characteristic K_x.
- **Conclusion**: **U** will possess similar characteristic U_x.

Bridge

You may not have realized it as you were studying Chapter 2 of *MCAT Organic Chemistry Review*, but isomerism offers a perfect illustration of the complexities within the concept of similarity. The key to understanding isomerism is to pay attention to the particular similarities and differences that make each isomeric relationship precisely what it is. For example, conformational isomers, which differ only in rotation around a σ bond, are much more alike than structural (constitutional) isomers in which the bonds are not even identical, which is why conformers tend to share so many more properties. On the CARS section, you'll be relating concepts rather than chemicals, but you'll still want to break down the specifics. *Reasoning Beyond the Text* questions become far more manageable if you can isolate the exact points of likeness that new ideas and claims share with passage information, as well as those places in which the two diverge.

Key Concept

An argument from analogy is a kind of justification in which the two pieces of evidence are the similarity between two terms and the known existence of a particular characteristic in one of the two. The conclusion is that the other unknown term will also possess the same or a similar characteristic.

This type of reasoning is employed regularly in biological contexts. For instance, Charles Darwin's explanation of the origin of new species is based on an analogy from agriculture and animal husbandry. If *artificial selection* can account for dramatic differences in the appearance of domesticated plants and animals over just a few generations, Darwin reasoned, then perhaps *natural selection* could account for speciation over longer stretches of time. Mapping onto the formal version above, **K** (the known) would be the crops and livestock found on farms, while **U** (the unknown) would be all the species in nature, and the *x* terms would concern the selectors that cause species divergence.

The strength of arguments from analogy can vary widely. An analogy will be weak if it depends on only one minor point of similarity between the known and the unknown or if it draws upon commonalities (regardless of quantity) that are irrelevant to the conclusion. Just like in genetics, in which a mutation to a noncoding region of the genome tends to have no consequences for the organism's phenotype, a point of contrast between a new scenario and the passage could be insignificant to the question at hand. For example, it would be a mistake to infer, as did many ancient cultures, that the sun and the moon are living creatures because they move across the sky like birds. Though celestial bodies and avian fauna share this superficial feature, the reasons behind their motion are vastly divergent, so the analogy does not hold.

Although analogies are often located within passages themselves (making them fair game for questions that would fall under the other categories), analogical reasoning is most often tested in CARS through the use of *Reasoning Beyond the Text* questions. Your task with these will be to isolate the known from the unknown and assess their corresponding points of analogy. There is no easy formula for judging how similar two situations are or for determining how relevant a point of commonality is for an analogy, but these are skills that will improve with additional CARS practice. As a general rule, the MCAT tends to ask about "deeper" points of analogy, going beneath surface characteristics to underlying structural similarities. So, if a question asks for an item analogous to a forged painting, the correct answer would more likely involve deception (such as a disguise or a lie) than artistic representation (such as a photograph or sculpture).

EXTRAPOLATION AND INTEGRATION

There are two basic ways in which analogical reasoning is employed in CARS. In one case, the passage provides the known term, with its various characteristics, and the question gives the new context that establishes the unknown. In such questions, you are being asked to apply, extend, or extrapolate the ideas from the passage to a new situation, so you can take the information from the passage as a given. Kaplan thus calls these Apply questions, as described in Chapter 11 of *MCAT CARS Review*.

Bridge

Reasoning Beyond the Text questions, described in Chapter 11 of *MCAT CARS Review*, make up 40 percent of the questions you'll see on Test Day. These questions share one common feature: asking for the connections between the passage and new information. Oftentimes, these questions focus on analogical arguments.

In the other case, you will have to integrate or incorporate new ideas into the passage, making a judgment about the effect that they would have. For these questions, the information from the text is subject to change, and so we treat it as though it were the unknown, while the question stem typically establishes the known entity. The key to answering these effectively will be understanding how the new information provided is analogous to evidence, refutations, or conclusions from the passage itself. Because this question type usually deals with strengthening and weakening arguments, Kaplan calls these Strengthen–Weaken (Beyond the Passage) questions, which, as you'll see, are closely tied to the Strengthen–Weaken (Within the Passage) type, featured in Chapter 10 of *MCAT CARS Review*.

Conclusion

So ends the discussion of a few useful formal applications of logic. Appreciating the general characteristics of conditionals and analogies, as well as the ways in which each argumentative form manifests itself in passages and questions, will clarify your thinking and garner you many additional points. Given your new grasp of logic, we can now turn to consideration of the passages one last time and to the additional depths of understanding that can be gleaned when we integrate rhetorical analysis from Chapter 2 of *MCAT CARS Review* with not only the keywords and Outline strategies from Chapters 3 and 4 but also with the tools of logic just showcased in Chapters 5 and 6.

CONCEPT AND STRATEGY SUMMARY

The Logic of Conditionals

- A **conditional** is a unidirectional relationship that exists between two terms.
  - Conditionals can be represented with language (*if* **X**, *then* **Y**), or symbols: **X → Y**.
  - The **antecedent** (**X**) can also be called a **sufficient condition**, **evidence** (in cases of justification), or **cause** (in cases of causation).
  - The **consequent** (**Y**) can also be called a **necessary condition**, **conclusion** (in cases of justification), or **effect** (in cases of causation).
- A **conditional claim** is true if it is impossible to have a true antecedent and a false consequent simultaneously.
- Operations of formal logic can be represented in a **truth table**.
- **Sufficiency** refers to the impossibility of having an antecedent without its consequent.
- **Necessity** refers to the idea that if the consequent is not true, then the antecedent is also not true.
  - Necessity can be illustrated as *if not Y, then not X* or ~**Y → ~X**.
  - This conditional can also be called the **contrapositive**.
  - The contrapositive is logically equivalent to the original conditional, but it carries a different connotation.

Applications of Conditionals

- One common application of conditionals is the **whole–parts relationship**.
  - One concept can be a part of another concept (the whole) in the conceptual domain.
  - One component or characteristic can be part of an object in the natural domain.
- **Justification** is the relationship of logical support between a piece of evidence and its conclusion.
- **Correlation** is the relationship of two events accompanying one another.
- **Causation** is the one-way relationship of the antecedent leading to the consequent (cause and effect).
- There are many ways of writing the same logical relationship in English.

Analogical Reasoning

- Argument from analogy uses the similarities between two things to argue for an additional commonality between them.

  ○ The **known** entity is the one with characteristics that have already been established.

  ○ The **unknown** entity is the one that is only partially understood.

- The evidence in an analogical argument is twofold, leading to a single conclusion:

  ○ One piece of evidence is that the known and unknown entities share similar corresponding characteristics.

  ○ The other evidence is that the known entity possesses some characteristic of interest.

  ○ The conclusion drawn from this evidence is that the unknown entity also possesses a similar, relevant characteristic.

- An analogy can be strengthened by greater similarity between the known and unknown.

  ○ The more points of similarity between the two, the stronger the analogy.

  ○ The more relevant (structural as opposed to superficial) the similarities between the two, the stronger the analogy.

  ○ The fewer relevant differences between the two, the stronger the analogy.

Understanding Passages

In This Chapter

Introduction

This chapter is a turning point in *MCAT Critical Analysis and Reasoning Skills Review*. Whereas the previous chapters focused on insights into rhetoric, the modes of reading, and keywords; the Kaplan Method for CARS Passages; and arguments and logic; the chapters that follow will focus on the Kaplan Method for CARS Questions and question types. This is the same transition you'll make many times on Test Day, as you shift from critically reading a passage to answering its questions. All of the strategies we've discussed thus far come together in this chapter, as we look at how the different passage elements can work together to improve your understanding of the passages you encounter in the *Critical Analysis and Reasoning Skills* (CARS) section. All the while, we are looking ahead to the real source of points: correctly answering the questions.

This chapter is broken down as follows. First, we'll examine some characteristic varieties of passages that you can expect to see on Test Day while considering a few common themes that exist in each variety. Second, we'll discuss the different kinds of support that are used in passages and how these relate to the varieties introduced. Both the passage variety and the types of support that are used feed into the same common goal, which we address at the end of this chapter: anticipating the questions that will be asked for a given passage. Anticipating the questions profoundly improves your speed and accuracy in the CARS section—it's much quicker and easier to answer a question you've been waiting for all along!

7.1 Varieties of Passages

While the AAMC lists ten different fields in the humanities and a dozen different fields in the social sciences, as shown in Table 7.1, most CARS passages can be classified into one of a handful of categories. While it's true that each discipline has its own distinctive characteristics, similar fields share certain tendencies. Being aware of these similarities can help shape your expectations about what a passage will include as you Scan it in the first step of the Kaplan Method for CARS Passages. Moreover, as we'll see when we return to these examples in the final section of this chapter, you can also use these common varieties to help us predict the types of questions likely to be asked.

Humanities	Social Sciences
Architecture	Anthropology
Art	Archaeology
Dance	Economics
Ethics	Education
Literature	Geography
Music	History
Philosophy	Linguistics
Popular Culture	Political Science
Religion	Population Health
Studies of Diverse Cultures*	Psychology
Theater	Sociology
	Studies of Diverse Cultures*

* Note: Studies of Diverse Cultures can be tested in both humanities and social sciences passages.

Table 7.1. Humanities and Social Sciences Disciplines in the CARS Section

In order to offer you a better sense of the kind of variation that passages can bring, but without overwhelming you with the full 500–600 words of actual CARS passages, we introduce in this chapter a series of four mini-passages, each of which is about half the length of an ordinary CARS passage. We'll look at a number of characteristics of passages in this chapter, using them as illustrations. In Chapters 9 through 11 of *MCAT CARS Review*, which analyze the various question types, we'll return to these passages with sample questions that mimic what you could expect to see on Test Day. These examples are certainly not exhaustive; many passages will blend characteristics of the different varieties, and some passages will not cleanly fit into any of them. The benefit of determining the variety of the passage is to enable you to do something you may do unconsciously in the science sections: set your expectations appropriately. In a passage on rate kinetics, you expect to see rate laws, rate-of-formation tables, and reaction mechanisms. You anticipate that the questions will ask you to determine a rate law using the tables and to consider topics like rate-limiting steps and catalysis. Similarly, you can set expectations about the trajectory of a CARS passage by knowing its variety and can anticipate what questions you'll see on that passage. These expectations allow you to navigate the passage more quickly and to start racking up points with correct answers.

HUMANITIES

Passages in the humanities tend to fall into two broad categories. The first category, which includes most of the passages from architecture, art, dance, literature, music, popular culture, and theater, could broadly be considered **Arts passages**. They tend to take a form like the following:

An Arts Passage

One of the first examples of the ascendance of abstraction in 20th-century art is the Dada movement, which Lowenthal dubbed "the groundwork to abstract art and sound poetry, a starting point for performance art, a prelude to postmodernism, an influence on pop art…and the movement that laid the foundation for surrealism." Dadaism was ultimately premised on a philosophical rejection of the dominant culture, which is to say the dominating culture of colonialist Europe. Not content with the violent exploitation of other peoples, the gaze of Europe's ruling factions once again turned inward, reigniting provincial disputes into the conflagration that came to be known by the Eurocentric epithet "World War I"—the European subcontinent apparently being the only part of the world that mattered.

The absurd destructiveness of the Great War was a natural prelude to the creative absurdity of Dada. Is it any wonder that the rejection of reason made manifest by senseless atrocities should lead to the embrace of irrationality and disorder among the West's subaltern artistic communities? Marcel Janco, one of the first Dadaists, cited this rationale: "We had lost confidence in our culture. Everything had to be demolished. We would begin again after the *tabula rasa*." Thus, we find the overturning of what was once considered art: a urinal becomes the *Fountain* after Marcel Duchamp signs it "R. Mutt" in 1917, the nonsense syllables of Hugo Ball and Kurt Schwitters transform into "sound poems," dancers in cardboard cubist costumes accompanied by foghorns and typewriters metamorphosize into the ballet *Parade*. Unsurprisingly, many commentators, including founding members, have described Dada as an "anti-art" movement. Notwithstanding such a designation, Dadaism has left a lasting imprint on modern Western art.

Sample Outline

P1. Dada (Author ++): early abstract art, originated in rejection of European culture (Author – –)

P2. WWI led to Dada's "creative absurdity"; example artworks

Goal: To discuss the impact, origins, and characteristics of Dadaism

Notice the heavy use of quotations from both artists and critics, the strong opinions evident in the passage's Author keywords, and the use of descriptive language to illustrate artistic examples. While not every Arts passage will take this form—literature passages, in particular, can show a lot of variation beyond these tendencies—many will.

Most of the other passages in the humanities fall into the second category, which includes ethics, philosophy, religion, and studies of diverse cultures and which might be called **Philosophical passages** more broadly. The following, from the field of ethics, is such a passage:

An Ethics Passage

The most prevalent argument against doctor-assisted suicide relies upon a distinction between *passive* and *active* euthanasia—in essence, the difference between killing someone and letting that person die. On this account, a physician is restricted by her Hippocratic oath to do no harm and thus cannot act in ways that would inflict the ultimate harm, death. In contrast, failing to resuscitate an individual who is dying is permitted because this would only be an instance of refraining from help and not a willful cause of harm. The common objection to this distinction, that it is vague and therefore difficult to apply, does not carry much weight. After all, applying ethical principles of *any sort* to the complexities of the world is an enterprise fraught with imprecision.

Rather, the fundamental problem with the distinction is that it is not an ethically relevant one, readily apparent in the following thought experiment. Imagine a terminally ill patient hooked up to an unusual sort of life support device, one that only functioned to prevent a separate "suicide machine" from administering a lethal injection so long as the doctor pressed a button on it once per day. Would there be any relevant difference between using the suicide machine directly and not using the prevention device? The intention of the doctor would be the same (fulfilling the patient's wish to die), and the effect would be the same (an injection causing the patient's death). The only variance here is the means by which the effect comes about, and this is not an ethical difference but merely a technical one.

Sample Outline

P1. "Most prevalent argument" against euthanasia assumes passive/active difference (vague is okay)

P2. Author: distinction is not ethically relevant (supported w/thought experiment)

Goal: To argue the distinction between passive and active euthanasia is not ethically relevant

Philosophical passages tend to be abstract and heavy on logic—the Descartes passage from Chapter 4 of *MCAT CARS Review* was another such example. They focus reader's memory or imagination, drawing on common experiences or thought experiments (as in the second paragraph of this passage).

Keep in mind that there will be plenty of humanities passages that mix characteristics of Arts and Philosophical passages, as well as some passages that don't properly fit in either category. Nevertheless, this distinction is useful (as we'll see below) for setting expectations about the kind of support that a passage will use as well as the types of questions that will accompany it.

SOCIAL SCIENCES

When it comes to the social sciences, some passages take what might be called a **Scientific** form, such as passages in anthropology, education, linguistics, population health, psychology, and sociology. Here's an example from psychology:

A Psychology Passage

There is no shortage of evidence for the existence of systemic biases in ordinary human reasoning. For instance, Kahneman and Tversky in their groundbreaking 1974 work proposed the existence of a heuristic—an error-prone shortcut in reasoning—known as "anchoring." In one of their most notable experiments, participants were exposed to the spin of a roulette wheel (specially rigged to land randomly on one of only two possible results) before being asked to guess what percent of United Nations member states were African. The half of the sample who had the roulette wheel stop at 65 guessed, on average, that 45% of the UN was African, while those with a result of 10 guessed only 25%, demonstrating that prior presentation of a random number otherwise unconnected to a quantitative judgment can still influence that judgment.

The anchoring effect has been observed on repeated other occasions, such as in Dan Ariely's experiment that used digits in Social Security numbers as an anchor for bids at an auction, and in the 1996 study by Wilson *et al*. that showed even awareness of the existence of anchoring bias is insufficient to mitigate its effects. The advertising industry has long been aware of this bias, the rationale for its frequent practice of featuring an "original" price before showing a "sale" price that is invariably reduced. Of course, anchoring is hardly alone among the defective tendencies in human reasoning; other systemic biases have also been experimentally identified, including loss aversion, the availability heuristic, and optimism bias.

Sample Outline

P1. Systemic biases in reasoning: ex. anchoring heuristic (evidence: Kahneman & Tversky)

P2. More evidence for anchoring (Ariely, Wilson et al.); other systemic biases

Goal: To present evidence for systemic biases in reasoning, especially anchoring

In this passage, the numbers should jump off the page, along with the heavy reference to empirical studies as support (discussed more below). The author's opinion is less glaring than in an Arts passage, but there are still indications of attitude with Author keywords like *groundbreaking* and *notable* in the first paragraph. In fact, a Scientific passage could come to look more like a passage in the *Psychological, Social, and Biological Foundations of Behavior* section.

The counterparts to Scientific passages are **Historical passages**, which include many examples from archaeology, economics, geography, history, political science, and studies of diverse cultures. Note that this type is far more variable than the others and can sometimes even look a little bit more like a humanities passage, such as in this example:

A History Passage

In 1941, an exuberant nationalist wrote: "We must accept wholeheartedly our duty and our opportunity as the most powerful and vital nation...to exert upon the world the full impact of our influence, for such purposes as we see fit and by such means as we see fit." If forced to guess the identity of the writer, many US citizens would likely suspect a German jingoist advocating for *Lebensraum*. In actuality, the sentiment was expressed by one of America's own: Henry Luce, the highly influential publisher of the magazines *Life*, *Time*, and *Fortune*. Luce sought to dub the 1900s the "American Century," calling upon the nation to pursue global hegemony as it slipped from the grasp of warring Old World empires. As a forecast of world history, Luce's pronouncement seems prescient—but is it justifiable as a normative stance?

Not all of Luce's contemporaries bought into his exceptionalist creed. Only a year later, Henry Wallace, vice president under FDR, insisted that no country had the "right to exploit other nations" and that "military [and] economic imperialism" were invariably immoral. It is a foundational assumption in ethics that the wrongness of an act is independent of the particular identity of the actor—individuals who pay no heed to moral consistency are justly condemned as hypocrites. So why should it be any different for nation-states? In accord with this principle, Wallace proselytized for "the century of the common man," for the furtherance of a "great revolution of the people," and for bringing justice and prosperity to all persons irrespective of accidents of birth. Sadly, Wallace never had the chance to lead the United States in this cosmopolitan direction; prior to Roosevelt's demise at the beginning of his fourth term, the vice presidency was handed to Harry Truman, a man whose narrow provincialism ensconced him firmly in Luce's camp. And with Truman came the ghastly atomic eradication of two Japanese cities, the dangerous precedent set by military action without congressional approval in Korea, and a Cold War with the Soviet Union that brought the world to the brink of nuclear destruction.

Sample Outline

P1. Luce: "American Century" = U.S. has right to influence world (Author: – – –)

P2. U.S. V.P. Wallace (+ + +) rejected Luce's idea, but replaced by Truman (– – –) who supported it

Goal: To describe Luce and Wallace's opposing views on U.S. power, favoring Wallace

Not all historical passages will be this heavily opinionated, but they will tend to draw on historical events and quotations from sources alive at the time of the events discussed. In passages in history, economics, and political science, you'll occasionally find empirical studies, which make them more like Scientific passages, or heavy theoretical discussions, which make them more Philosophical.

7.2 Support in Passages

Because a majority of questions in the CARS section will have some connection to logical support, it's essential to understand the different kinds of support that can be found in CARS passages.

CATEGORIES OF SUPPORT

Unsupported Claims

Authors say a lot of different things in CARS passages—a single long paragraph could potentially contain a dozen distinct claims. Consequently, not every assertion they make will be backed with evidence. You can recognize unsupported claims in a passage because they lack any logical connections to other parts of the passage, whether through Logic keywords or implied through context. If these claims are uncontroversial (*the sky is blue*, *2 + 2 = 4*, *the heart pumps blood*), then there really isn't a problem with leaving the claim unsupported, and you're not likely to be asked about it in a question. Watch out, though, when you find an unsupported claim that is not widely accepted—anything that either you don't believe personally or that you know that some people might not believe. Those are the types of unsupported claims most likely to be asked about in a question.

Real World

In clinical medicine, the different types of research protocols can be placed in a hierarchy based on the strength of their evidence. Double-blind, randomized controlled studies give the strongest possible evidence, followed by systematic reviews (meta-analyses), cohort and case–control studies, case series, and expert opinion. Some of these research protocols are discussed in Chapter 11 of *MCAT Physics and Math Review*.

Bridge

Deductive (top-down) reasoning starts from a set of general rules and draws conclusions from the information given. This is different from inductive (bottom-up) reasoning, which seeks to create a theory via generalizations from specific instances. These problem-solving patterns are discussed in Chapter 4 of *MCAT Behavioral Sciences Review*.

Bridge

In Chapter 6 of *MCAT CARS Review*, we presented analogical reasoning as a set of two pieces of evidence and a conclusion:
- **Evidence: K** and **U** share similar corresponding characteristics (K_1 and U_1, K_2 and U_2, K_3 and U_3, and so on);
- **Evidence: K** possesses characteristic K_x;
- **Conclusion: U** will possess similar characteristic U_x;
where K is a well-established entity and U is an entity that is only partially understood.

Empirical Evidence

Whenever an author appeals to experience, particularly in the context of scientific studies, he is using empirical evidence. While anecdotes, historical accounts, and case studies draw upon experience, these are limited in value because they only represent single cases. In other forms of empirical evidence, such as surveys, statistical analyses, and controlled experiments, variables can be isolated, and evidence can be gathered from looking at a wide swath of experience.

Experiments are most likely to be used as support in Scientific passages, although occasionally they will appear in a Historical passage or even a Philosophical passage. When you see them, be sure to identify the specific claim that they are being used to support because this is a common question. The example Psychology passage earlier used primarily this kind of support.

Logical Appeals

In Chapter 2 of *MCAT CARS Review*, logical appeals were introduced as appeals to *logos*, the Greek word from which *logic* is derived. If a claim is supported logically, the author makes deductions on the basis of how concepts are defined and related to one another. For example, the **contrapositive** is logically supported by the conditional claim that it comes from, as discussed in Chapter 6 of *MCAT CARS Review*.

Two other examples of logical appeals are analogies and the elimination of alternative possibilities. Analogical reasoning is employed whenever two things known to be alike in (at least) one respect are concluded to be alike in a different respect for which there may not be direct evidence. For instance, if an author argues that chimpanzees are more self-aware than other primates because they have larger brains, then she is likely making an analogy between chimpanzees and humans—both have brains that are larger than other primates (for humans, considerably more so), but it's hard to gauge precisely how "self-aware" chimpanzees can be directly, so the analogy gives support where no other might be found.

The most classic example of eliminating the alternatives is the **reduction to absurdity** (*reductio ad absurdum*), in which the opposite of what the author is trying to prove is shown to have logical consequences that are ridiculous or even self-contradictory. Another example is when alternative hypotheses are ruled out by considering their weaknesses. Technically speaking, eliminating the alternatives only helps to support the author's position if all of the other possibilities are ruled out—this is easy in the case of a reduction to absurdity but extremely difficult when attempting to, say, explain the cause of a phenomenon.

Logical appeals are most likely to be found in Philosophical passages, like the earlier Ethics passage, where they predominate, but they make limited appearances in the other types of passages as well.

Authority

Whenever an author draws on another person or text to support his claims, that author is appealing to authority. This is a way of making an appeal to *ethos*, as discussed in Chapter 2 of *MCAT CARS Review*. Occasionally, authors will try to demonstrate their own expertise and use that as a basis to bolster their other arguments, but far more often authors draw on outside sources, using paraphrases and direct quotations.

The level of support this offers varies depending on the credibility of the authority. **Primary sources**—for instance, a firsthand account of a historic event or the novel of a writer being discussed—provide the greatest level of support (short of having the experience itself). **Secondary sources**—that is, analyses and commentaries on primary sources (or other secondary sources)—are more dubious in value, and their value varies based on the expertise of the authority being cited. If the individual cited is discussing an area in which she has expertise (and is widely believed to have expertise), then a secondary source provides a significant level of support.

The appeal to authority is extremely common in Arts and Historical passages as in the examples earlier, and it may also be found in some Philosophical passages, especially those in religion.

Appeals to the Reader

Many authors will try to use their readers to help ground their arguments by beginning from starting points that their intended audiences are likely to share. For instance, as first addressed in Chapter 2 of *MCAT CARS Review*, whenever an author asks a rhetorical question, it's expected that the reader will have one specific response that the author had in mind when writing it (usually just *yes* or *no*). Also included in this broad category would be emotional appeals (appeals to *pathos*), in which charged language or colorful description is supposed to evoke particular responses from the audience.

Other times, authors try to rely upon the memories or imaginations of their readers. When authors support a claim by drawing on an everyday experience that the reader can recollect, or through a hypothetical situation or thought experiment, they're actually making the reader do most of the work for them. Whenever authors draw upon a relatively noncontroversial claim—something that everyone in the audience is likely to believe, something that will mesh with the reader's intuition—they are engaging in this kind of support. Note that such a claim still

Bridge

Lawrence Kohlberg's theory of moral reasoning provides a great example of individuals sharing the same beliefs, but with very different reasons for holding these beliefs. The Heinz dilemma, presented in Chapter 6 of *MCAT Behavioral Sciences Review*, is a classic example: depending on whether a person's reasoning is preconventional, conventional, or postconventional, he may justify his answer (whether it is right or wrong for an individual to steal a high–profit margin medication he cannot afford for his terminally ill wife) with completely different logic.

counts as support even if the audience members have starkly different reasons for believing it.

The thought experiment in the Ethics passage and the rhetorical questions in the Arts and History passages are examples of this type of appeal. The morally loaded language found in the latter is undeniably an appeal to *pathos*.

Faulty Support

If an author backs up a controversial claim with another claim that is similarly controversial, that author is simply using one assertion to back another. Unless that assertion is itself supported in some way (through one of the other types discussed here), then this kind of support is extremely weak at best. It's practically like leaving a claim unsupported.

Appeals in this category would include the wide variety of **specious reasoning**—arguments that superficially seem plausible but are actually flawed. Examples draw upon fallacies in reasoning like *ad hominem* attacks (attacking a person's character), making hasty generalizations from insufficient data, applying assumptions about a group to individual cases (stereotyping), and refuting straw-man positions (extreme versions of a view that no one seriously holds). It's relatively rare that such errors in reasoning appear in CARS passages, so if you notice one, expect to see a question on it.

7.3 Anticipating Questions

Let's return once again to the four mini-passages from the first section, but this time view them with an eye toward the kinds of questions that would probably be included with each on Test Day.

An Arts Passage

One of the first examples of the ascendance of abstraction in 20th-century art is the Dada movement, which Lowenthal dubbed "the groundwork to abstract art and sound poetry, a starting point for performance art, a prelude to postmodernism, an influence on pop art…and the movement that laid the foundation for surrealism." Dadaism was ultimately premised on a philosophical rejection of the dominant culture, which is to say the dominating culture of colonialist Europe. Not content with the violent exploitation of other peoples, the gaze of Europe's ruling factions once again turned inward, reigniting provincial disputes into the conflagration that came to be known by the Eurocentric epithet "World War I"—the European subcontinent apparently being the only part of the world that mattered.

The absurd destructiveness of the Great War was a natural prelude to the creative absurdity of Dada. Is it any wonder that the rejection of reason made manifest by senseless atrocities should lead to the embrace of irrationality and disorder among the West's subaltern artistic communities? Marcel Janco, one of the first Dadaists, cited this rationale: "We had lost confidence in our culture. Everything had to be demolished. We would begin again after the *tabula rasa*." Thus, we find the overturning of what was once considered art: a urinal becomes the *Fountain* after Marcel Duchamp signs it "R. Mutt" in 1917, the nonsense syllables of Hugo Ball and Kurt Schwitters transform into "sound poems," dancers in cardboard cubist costumes accompanied by foghorns and typewriters metamorphosize into the ballet *Parade*. Unsurprisingly, many commentators, including founding members, have described Dada as an "anti-art" movement. Notwithstanding such a designation, Dadaism has left a lasting imprint on modern Western art.

Because this passage is relatively heavy on opinion, expect to see questions that require identifying what the author would agree or disagree with. So, for instance, it's clear this author has a negative opinion of European colonialism and warfare, but a positive opinion of Dada—which is not so surprising because this art is supposedly a rejection of those tendencies in European culture. A more difficult opinion to untangle might be the one at the very end: the author attributes the view to *many commentators* that Dadaism is *"anti-art,"* yet the author uses a Difference keyword (*Notwithstanding*) to signal disagreement with that conclusion, which is consistent with the author's use of the word *art* to refer to Dada, such as in the very first sentence.

This passage is also abundant in details, so expect Detail questions, described in Chapter 9 of *MCAT CARS Review*, which require you to comb through the passage searching for particular bits from the text.

What this passage lacks is much in the way of support, aside from quotations presumably coming from an art scholar in the first paragraph and an artist, *one of the first Dadaists*, in the second. Because you can still expect to see questions on reasoning accompanying any passage, it's quite likely that they'll bring in new elements to account for the relative dearth of evidence.

An Ethics Passage

The most prevalent argument against doctor-assisted suicide relies upon a distinction between *passive* and *active* euthanasia—in essence, the difference between killing someone and letting that person die. On this account, a physician is restricted by her Hippocratic oath to do no harm and thus cannot act in ways that would inflict the ultimate harm, death. In contrast, failing to resuscitate an individual who is dying is permitted because this

Bridge

Passages with a lack of support or argumentation are likely to include *Reasoning Beyond the Text* questions, which bring in a new element of information and ask you to apply the information in the passage to a new scenario (Apply questions) or ask how the new information would impact the passage (Strengthen–Weaken (Beyond the Text) questions). These question types are discussed in Chapter 11 of *MCAT CARS Review*.

would only be an instance of refraining from help and not a willful cause of harm. The common objection to this distinction, that it is vague and therefore difficult to apply, does not carry much weight. After all, applying ethical principles of *any sort* to the complexities of the world is an enterprise fraught with imprecision.

Rather, the fundamental problem with the distinction is that it is not an ethically relevant one, readily apparent in the following thought experiment. Imagine a terminally ill patient hooked up to an unusual sort of life support device, one that only functioned to prevent a separate "suicide machine" from administering a lethal injection so long as the doctor pressed a button on it once per day. Would there be any relevant difference between using the suicide machine directly and not using the prevention device? The intention of the doctor would be the same (fulfilling the patient's wish to die), and the effect would be the same (an injection causing the patient's death). The only variance here is the means by which the effect comes about, and this is not an ethical difference but merely a technical one.

This passage repeatedly uses an Opposition keyword, *distinction*, so expect to see questions requiring you to understand the basic conceptual difference between active and passive euthanasia. The author's characterization of this as *not an ethical difference but merely a technical one* at the end of the passage is particularly likely to be important because it includes an additional opposition: ethical *vs.* technical differences.

The numerous Logic keywords mean you can also anticipate questions that ask about the author's argumentative structure; called Strengthen–Weaken (Within the Passage) questions, these are discussed in Chapter 10 of *MCAT CARS Review*. Notice the author's use of an appeal to the reader's imagination by means of a thought experiment—this is definitely ripe for questioning.

A Psychology Passage

There is no shortage of evidence for the existence of systemic biases in ordinary human reasoning. For instance, Kahneman and Tversky in their groundbreaking 1974 work proposed the existence of a heuristic—an error-prone shortcut in reasoning—known as "anchoring." In one of their most notable experiments, participants were exposed to the spin of a roulette wheel (specially rigged to land randomly on one of only two possible results) before being asked to guess what percent of United Nations member states were African. The half of the sample who had the roulette wheel stop at 65 guessed, on average, that 45% of the UN was African, while those with a result of 10 guessed only 25%, demonstrating that prior presentation of a random number otherwise unconnected to a quantitative judgment can still influence that judgment.

The anchoring effect has been observed on repeated other occasions, such as in Dan Ariely's experiment that used digits in Social Security numbers as an anchor for bids at an auction, and in the 1996 study by Wilson *et al.* that showed even awareness of the existence of anchoring bias is insufficient to mitigate its effects. The advertising industry has long been aware of this bias, the rationale for its frequent practice of featuring an "original" price before showing a "sale" price that is invariably reduced. Of course, anchoring is hardly alone among the defective tendencies in human reasoning; other systemic biases have also been experimentally identified, including loss aversion, the availability heuristic, and optimism bias.

This passage focuses on a particular phenomenon, so you can expect to see questions asking about what the term *anchoring* means or for examples of it. Because the author never explicitly defines the word, and you have to figure it out from the experiments described, you're especially likely to see questions about it.

In addition, you should also anticipate questions asking about what the cited experiments actually show and what assertions they support. These questions would fall broadly into the *Reasoning Within the Text* category.

A History Passage

In 1941, an exuberant nationalist wrote: "We must accept wholeheartedly our duty and our opportunity as the most powerful and vital nation…to exert upon the world the full impact of our influence, for such purposes as we see fit and by such means as we see fit." If forced to guess the identity of the writer, many US citizens would likely suspect a German jingoist advocating for *Lebensraum*. In actuality, the sentiment was expressed by one of America's own: Henry Luce, the highly influential publisher of the magazines *Life*, *Time*, and *Fortune*. Luce sought to dub the 1900s the "American Century," calling upon the nation to pursue global hegemony as it slipped from the grasp of warring Old World empires. As a forecast of world history, Luce's pronouncement seems prescient—but is it justifiable as a normative stance?

Not all of Luce's contemporaries bought into his exceptionalist creed. Only a year later, Henry Wallace, vice president under FDR, insisted that no country had the "right to exploit other nations" and that "military [and] economic imperialism" were invariably immoral. It is a foundational assumption in ethics that the wrongness of an act is independent of the particular identity of the actor—individuals who pay no heed to moral consistency are justly condemned as hypocrites. So why should it be any different for nation-states? In accord with this principle, Wallace proselytized for "the century of the common man," for the furtherance of a "great revolution

Bridge

When a passage uses a term repeatedly without explicitly defining it, expect a question that asks you for this definition. These questions, appropriately called Definition-in-Context questions, are discussed in Chapter 9 of *MCAT CARS Review*.

of the people," and for bringing justice and prosperity to all persons irrespective of accidents of birth. Sadly, Wallace never had the chance to lead the United States in this cosmopolitan direction; prior to Roosevelt's demise at the beginning of his fourth term, the vice presidency was handed to Harry Truman, a man whose narrow provincialism ensconced him firmly in Luce's camp. And with Truman came the ghastly atomic eradication of two Japanese cities, the dangerous precedent set by military action without congressional approval in Korea, and a Cold War with the Soviet Union that brought the world to the brink of nuclear destruction.

When two opposing views are presented, as in this passage, you can be sure that you'll get questions asking you about one of the views or requiring you to contrast them. You could see straightforward questions asking you about who says what, about whom the author favors (as noted in our sample outline earlier, it's clearly Wallace in the passage), or about the assumptions implicit in each view.

The author's strong opinion is also ripe for questions, just as was the case in the Arts passage. Although many authors are fairly moderate, a substantial minority do take more overt positions, heavily employing Positive, Negative, and Extreme Author keywords. While you may not get an explicit question asking about the extreme view, you can at least expect to use your knowledge of the author's attitude to eliminate inappropriate answer choices.

Conclusion

And so our discussion of passages draws to a close. The skills that you've gained in learning how to dissect passages—from understanding rhetorical elements to using keywords and reading critically, from the Kaplan Method for CARS Passages to argumentation and formal logic, from recognizing varieties of passages to anticipating questions—will serve you well not only on the MCAT but in medical school and as a physician. While reading a CARS passage, we use keywords to guide our reading and determine how information is put together; we draw inferences and set expectations for where the author is likely to go with a given argument; we anticipate the likely questions we'll be asked. In medicine, we must *listen* critically to our patients, determining how the complaints they describe fit together. *I've just been feeling "blah,"* your patient may say to you some day. *I feel tired, my skin's been dry, I've been putting on some weight, and I always feel cold.* From this information, you may infer that the patient likely has hypothyroidism. You then set expectations for some of the other signs and symptoms the patient may have, which guide your physical exam: Does the patient have a goiter (a swelling of the thyroid gland)? What about delayed deep tendon reflexes? Perhaps a slow pulse rate? And you anticipate the questions the patient will ask you—*What does this mean for me? Do*

Key Concept

Passages that include a number of differing opinions will usually be accompanied by questions that ask about the differences between those opinions, who holds which opinions, or the assumptions implicit in the various opinions.

I have to take medication for this? Does this put me at risk for anything else? In the end, the *Critical Analysis and Reasoning Skills* section gets its name because it tests your ability not to comprehend dance theory, musicology, archaeology, and linguistics, but to understand how to analyze and reason through complex information delivered verbally.

Passages are only a part of the picture, though. While we need to read the passage to gain information, the real points come from the questions. In the next four chapters, we shift our focus to these questions, starting with the Kaplan Method for CARS Questions and then focusing on the major types of questions that fall into the three AAMC categories: *Foundations of Comprehension*, *Reasoning Within the Text*, and *Reasoning Beyond the Text*.

CONCEPT AND STRATEGY SUMMARY

Varieties of Passages

- **Humanities passages** include topics from architecture, art, dance, ethics, literature, music, philosophy, popular culture, religion, studies of diverse cultures, and theater. Many passages in the humanities can be considered Arts passages or Philosophical passages.

  - **Arts passages** tend to include strong opinions, quotations, and descriptive language to illustrate examples.

  - **Philosophical passages** tend to be abstract and heavy on logic, focusing heavily on concepts and relations between them; they often appeal to the reader's memory or imagination.

- **Social sciences passages** include topics from anthropology, archaeology, economics, education, geography, history, linguistics, political science, population health, psychology, sociology, and studies of diverse cultures. Many passages in the social sciences can be considered Scientific passages or Historical passages.

  - **Scientific passages** tend to include empirical studies and more subtle author opinions.

  - **Historical passages** tend to draw on historical events and quotations from sources alive at the time; they may include empirical studies or theoretical evidence, which can make them similar to the other passage varieties.

Support in Passages

- **Unsupported claims** are assertions that lack evidence. If the claim is uncontroversial, no evidence is generally needed. If the claim is controversial, however, the absence of evidence makes the claim questionable—and likely to be tested.

- **Empirical evidence** includes surveys, statistical analyses, and controlled experiments, although it can also include anecdotes, historical accounts, and case studies. Empirical evidence is most frequently used in Scientific passages.

- **Logical appeals** include formation of the contrapositive, analogical reasoning, and elimination of alternative possibilities.

- **Appeals to authority** include references to outside sources, paraphrases, and direct quotations. This technique is commonly used in Arts and Historical passages.

  - **Primary sources** give the greatest level of support and are first-hand accounts directly from the time period or situation being discussed.

  - **Secondary sources** provide less support and include commentaries on or explanations for primary sources (or other secondary sources).

- **Appeals to the reader** include rhetorical questions, emotional appeals (using charged language or colorful description to evoke an emotional response from the audience), and appeals to memory or imagination.

- **Faulty support** comes in many forms, but it includes attacking a person's character, making generalizations, stereotyping, and refuting straw-man positions. Faulty support is rare, but—when present—is often tested.

Anticipating Questions

- In general, it is important to anticipate the questions that will be associated with a given passage because doing so increases your speed and accuracy when moving through the question set.

- Passages that are abundant in details often contain Detail questions.

- Passages that use a new term often contain Definition-in-Context questions.

- Passages that are heavy on opinion often contain Inference questions.

- Passages that contain multiple opinions often contain questions that require distinguishing or classifying different opinions.

- Passages that are heavy on Logic keywords or empirical evidence often contain Strengthen–Weaken (Within the Passage) questions.

- Passages that lack support will often ask for this support through *Reasoning Beyond the Text* questions.

Question and Answer Strategy

In This Chapter

Introduction

Thus far, this book has examined the multifarious aspects of *Critical Analysis and Reasoning Skills* (CARS) passages. You've learned about their rhetorical characteristics in Chapter 2 and their logical structure in Chapters 5 and 6. You've seen how to approach them strategically, using the Keywords introduced in Chapter 3 and following the Kaplan Method for CARS Passages elaborated upon in Chapter 4. In Chapter 7, these threads were brought together as we discussed what understanding passages really means.

We now begin to consider question stems and answer choices. We start by outlining the Kaplan Method for MCAT Questions, as tailored to the CARS section. Subsequently, we look at the recurring traps that the testmakers set for the unwary student, which we call Wrong Answer Pathologies. In the final portion, we'll consider the counterpart to pathologies: patterns common in correct answers.

8.1 Kaplan Method for CARS Questions

In Chapter 4 of *MCAT CARS Review*, we saw how the general Kaplan Method for tackling MCAT passages could be refined to tailor the needs of the CARS section. In this section, we'll do the same with our question method, which takes the basic form shown in Figure 8.1.

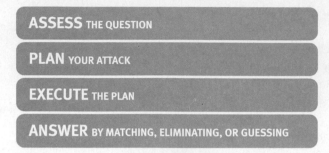

Figure 8.1. The Kaplan Method for Questions

This same four-step approach should be used on all questions on the MCAT—in both the *Critical Analysis and Reasoning Skills* section and the science sections. The CARS-specific version is shown in Figure 8.2.

ASSESS THE QUESTION

- Read the question, **NOT** the answers
- Identify the question type and difficulty
- Decide to attack *now* or *later*

PLAN YOUR ATTACK

- Establish the task set by the question type
- Find clues in the stem on where to research
- Navigate the passage using your Outline

EXECUTE THE PLAN

- Predict what you can about the answer
- Set expectations for wrong choices
- Be flexible if your first Plan flops

ANSWER BY MATCHING, ELIMINATING, OR GUESSING

- Find a match for your prediction, or
- Eliminate the three wrong options, or
- Make an educated guess

Figure 8.2. The Kaplan Method for Questions in CARS

Note: The Kaplan Method for CARS Questions, as well as the Kaplan Method for CARS Passages, CARS Question Types, and Wrong Answer Pathologies are included as tear-out sheets in the back of this book.

ASSESS

You might notice that the first step of the question method is similar to the Scan step of the Kaplan Method for CARS Passages. This is not a coincidence but rather a consequence of the timing constraints posed by the section. Because every question is worth the same number of points, there's no reason to get derailed by any one of them. Be honest with yourself: at least a few questions on each section are so difficult that you're likely to get them wrong no matter how many minutes you spend on them. Wouldn't it be better to recognize which questions those are right away so you can instead use that precious time where it will actually pay off?

Toward that end, your first task with any question will be to read the stem, and only the stem, for the sake of deciding either to work on it *now* or to triage (to use an apt medical metaphor) and save it for *later*. Assessing the difficulty will be easier if you can identify the **question type**. The three large **categories** that the AAMC uses were discussed in Chapter 1 of *MCAT CARS Review*, but through extensive research of all released MCAT material, we've discovered that almost all *Foundations of Comprehension* questions fall into one of four types. We've also found that the *Reasoning Within the Text* and *Reasoning Beyond the Text* categories can each be split into two predominant types with assorted others appearing rarely. Determining the question type will make devising and Executing a Plan much easier, which is why we devote the next three chapters to the types and their unique strategic concerns.

Why avoid looking at the answer choices? The primary reason is that most of them are wrong. If you glance at just one of them, for instance, it's three times more likely to be incorrect than correct and could seriously mislead you about the question. Inexperienced test takers immediately jump to the answers, and the AAMC punishes them for it by wording wrong options seductively. Selecting the first answer that looks good without first formulating a Plan is just a recipe for failure. Thus, until you get in the habit of ignoring the answers entirely until the Answer step, use your hand or a sticky note to cover them up whenever you start to work on a question.

PLAN

Once you've decided to attack a question, it's time to Plan your attack. First, be clear about what the question requires of you—what we call the **task**. Simpler question types like Main Idea and Definition-in-Context always involve one specific task (recognizing the big picture and explaining the meaning of part of the text as used in the passage, respectively), and even the more complex question types only have a small number of common objectives. An example is Apply questions, almost all of which involve one of three tasks: gauging the author's response, predicting a likely outcome, or finding a good example (as described in Chapter 11 of *MCAT CARS Review*).

In the journey to a correct answer, the task is your destination. To get to where you're headed, you need to know where you're starting from. Thus, the other major aspect of the Plan step is to determine where you'll find the information that you

Real World

Think of question typing as being like presenting diagnoses. In medical school, you will learn the appropriate steps to undertake if a patient presents with chest pain, abdominal pain, a severe headache, confusion, and so on. The ten question types should be thought of as the "presentation" of the question, which determines the appropriate steps to take through the rest of the Kaplan Method for CARS Questions.

MCAT Expertise

To avoid getting seduced by wrong answer choices, only scroll down far enough to read the question stem; leave the answer choices off-screen until you're ready for the Answer step. This will save you significant time and effort because you will avoid putting active consideration toward (and possibly being misled by!) the three wrong answer choices.

MCAT Expertise

If you ever find yourself scanning the passage to find an answer choice, you're doing it wrong! The information you need for the answer is often in your Outline; even if not, using your Outline to determine where in the passage to look for the answer means that you'll usually scan—at most—one paragraph of text.

need to answer the question. Note that there are only four viable sources of information on Test Day: the *question stem*, the *passage*, your *Outline*, and your *memory*.

It's rare, but occasionally you'll find that the stem gives you everything you need to answer the question. In other cases, the relevant info might be fresh in your mind, although human memory is notoriously faulty, and it doesn't hurt to check another source. This is one reason why it's so valuable to create an Outline as you read; it serves as a memory aid, capturing important aspects of the text that could slip your mind. In fact, sometimes the Outline is the only place you'll need to check, saving you the trouble of researching the passage. For instance, with Main Idea questions, the author's Goal in your Outline is usually all you'll need to examine. Not every question on the CARS section requires rereading the text: if a simple Plan yields immediate success, accept it and don't second guess yourself.

Whenever you're facing less straightforward tasks, though, it's advised that you reread at least part of the passage. Stems almost always contain clues hinting at where to research, taking one of three forms:

- Paragraph or sentence references
- Direct quotations
- Paraphrases

Sometimes paragraph numbers will be listed in parentheses, or you'll see a phrase like *the final sentence of the passage*, which makes location a breeze. The other clues may be harder to work with. Keep in mind that not all quotations taken from the passage will be surrounded by quote marks, particularly if only a single word or short phrase is mentioned; these brief terms are sometimes italicized but may appear without any embellishment at all. Also, keep in mind that shorter quotations could actually appear in multiple paragraphs. Although mercifully rare, paraphrases of passage claims without additional clues can be especially tricky: always remember that stems can use synonyms instead of the author's original language. A good Outline will help you find the paragraph that contains the information when you are working from a less direct clue.

Once you've figured out where to go in the passage, you'll want to make sure you cast a large enough net to find what you need. While the necessary information is often found directly in the portion of the passage that the stem points to, not infrequently you will find that the answer is in the surrounding text, in sentences immediately before or after. As a general rule of thumb, Plan to start rereading one sentence before the reference and to stop one sentence after.

What should your Plan be if you can't locate the clues or need to contend with vague questions that lack them entirely? Typically such questions are best to try later, at the very end of a passage set, after you've researched the other questions and already reread some of the text. You may find that by the time you return to it, the effort you put into other questions ended up revealing an unhelpful question stem's correct answer. When you do attempt these questions, process of elimination will usually end up being the best Plan.

EXECUTE

Every question has exactly one correct answer but typically will have more than one way to reach it. Indeed, the only difference between discovering the one correct answer and ruling out the three wrong ones is that the latter approach usually takes more time; the result is identical. Consequently, you want to strive for the quickest approach, but be flexible so that if Plan A fails, you have Plans B and C to fall back on.

In the Plan step for most questions, you'll identify where you need to reread (in your Outline or in the passage itself). Keep in mind the task of the particular question type as you now Execute the Plan and look over your Outline or the text again. Here, unlike with your first strategic reading of the passage (discussed in Chapter 4 of *MCAT CARS Review*), it's okay to reread the crucial sentences a few times if you need to because points are now on the line. In most cases, Plan A is to use the text to predict everything that you can about the correct answer, while Plan B is to set analogous expectations about what would rule out choices. The more specific these dual expectations, the easier it will be to isolate the answer.

For greater specificity in Planning and Executing an attack, see the strategy portion of the discussion for each of the question types covered in Chapters 9 through 11 of *MCAT CARS Review*. Where you look for information, as well as the way in which you approach rereading (including which keywords you pay attention to), will vary depending on the task.

ANSWER

All that remains now is to select the correct Answer. Scan the choices, and if you see an item that closely resembles what you expected, reread every word of that answer choice carefully to make sure it says precisely what you think it does. Then, select it and move on to the next question. At that point, *reading the other choices will not be worth your time*—be confident that you've Answered the question when you find a near-perfect match. When a good match is not available, *then* elimination is always an option.

That said, don't feel that you immediately need to resort to process of elimination if you read one answer choice and discover that the correct answer is going to take a completely different form than you first predicted. Part of being flexible is being able to revise your initial Plan, to set new expectations if the answer choices point you in that direction. The answer choices could technically be considered a fifth source of information, but keep in mind that they include a lot of misinformation and so should be treated with caution.

For example, a question stem may ask for a claim that undermines the author's thesis, a classic Strengthen–Weaken (Within the Passage) task, as described in Chapter 10 of *MCAT CARS Review*. For such a question, you may go into the answer choices expecting that the answer is a refutation mentioned in the passage. As soon as you read choice (A), though, you discover it's something entirely new, never even hinted at by the author. As you'll learn in Chapter 11 of *MCAT CARS Review*, such questions fall into the related Strengthen–Weaken (Beyond the Passage) type instead. Before moving on to read choice (B), you should think about whether choice (A) answers the question in a way you didn't anticipate. If so, use it to help you alter your expectations. Avoid the temptation to abandon the critical thinking you performed during the Execute step by reading the remaining three answer choices. Instead, formulate a new prediction and find a match among the three remaining answer choices.

Sometimes the question stem just doesn't give you very much to work with, and on other occasions you'll search through the answers but find no likely match. In these cases, you will have to use process of elimination, which may require multiple returns to the text as you research each choice individually. If you were able to set expectations during the Execute step for wrong choices, however, less additional research will be required. When evaluating choices, remember that the answer choices will sometimes vary the language used in the passage. Don't rule out a choice just because the wording is not quite what you anticipated; consistency of concepts matters more than identical terminology. Keep in mind that an answer only requires one major flaw for elimination, so the Wrong Answer Pathologies described below can greatly expedite the process.

When all else fails, you can fall back on educated guessing. Eliminate whatever you can and then go with your gut among the remaining options. Never make a blind guess unless you're completely out of time and need to fill in an answer choice. Even crossing off just one wrong answer will increase your chances of randomly choosing the correct one by 33 percent. Crossing off two wrong answers will double your chances. If possible, work on any unanswered questions for the passage and see if that effort allows you to return to rule out additional wrong options.

8.2 Wrong Answer Pathologies

The AAMC has designed the CARS section to be a fair test of critical thinking skills. The need for fairness is great news because it means that the questions won't play tricks on you! There will never be a question with two correct answer choices

MCAT Expertise

If you read a question stem and it doesn't give you very much to work with, don't just say *I don't know* and jump straight to the answer choices. Use your Outline to remember the main themes of the passage and then use those themes to help with process of elimination. This will help you avoid being distracted by answer choices that are seductive but that do not fit into the passage.

MCAT Expertise

Should I compare answer choices? Your default assumption should be that only one answer choice is flawless and that the others contain at least one flaw each, sufficient for ruling them out. However, you may occasionally find questions containing superlatives (*strongest challenge*, *most supported*, *best example*, and so on) in which you need to compare two or more answers that have the same effect but to different degrees. When making such comparisons, don't assume that an extreme answer is necessarily wrong, especially if the question stem includes the words *if true* or similar language. A stronger answer that nevertheless produces the desired outcome would be the correct choice.

or one in which all of the options are wrong. Each question you encounter on Test Day will have one and only one right answer and three that are incorrect for at least one reason. Even better, there can only be so many of these reasons: in fact, a few of them are found so frequently that you can treat them like recurring signs and symptoms of answer choice "illness." Naturally, we call them **Wrong Answer Pathologies**.

A choice only needs one fatal flaw to be worth eliminating, but often wrong answer options have many issues, so don't necessarily be alarmed if you ruled out a wrong answer for a different reason than the one mentioned in a practice question's explanation. In addition to having some occasional overlap, the following list of pathologies is not meant to be exhaustive; it only includes the four patterns we've identified as the most common through researching all of the released MCAT material. In the Kaplan Method for CARS Questions just detailed, pathologies function as recurring expectations for wrong answers, which you can assume fit for most of the questions you encounter (with a few significant departures noted below).

Note: The Wrong Answer Pathologies, as well as the Kaplan Method for CARS Passages, Kaplan Method for CARS Questions, and CARS Question Types are included as tear-out sheets in the back of this book.

FAULTY USE OF DETAIL (FUD)

The testmakers will often include accurate reflections of passage details in wrong answers, primarily to appeal to those students who jump at the familiar language. What makes the use of a detail "faulty" is that it simply doesn't answer the question posed. It may be too specific for a question that requires a general answer, or it may be that the detail comes from the wrong part of the passage. Even if a choice comes from the right paragraph, the detail cited might not be relevant to the question posed, which is often the case in Strengthen–Weaken (Within the Passage) questions. A thorough prediction makes catching these FUDs much easier.

OUT OF SCOPE (OS)

With the noteworthy exception of *Reasoning Beyond the Text* questions (for which this pathology does not apply), an answer choice that is outside the scope of the passage will inevitably be wrong. Typically, such answers will be on topic but will bring in some element that the text does not discuss. For instance, if an author never makes comparisons when discussing different ideas, an Out of Scope answer choice might involve the author ranking two or more concepts. Another common OS pattern is the suggestion that a view was the first of its kind or the most influential, when the author entirely avoids discussing its historical origins or relative popularity. Keep in mind that information can be unstated by the passage but not count as Out of Scope,

Key Concept

Wrong answer pathologies are the most frequent patterns found in incorrect answer choices. They are so common that you'll find at least one in just about every CARS question and even in many of the questions in the three science sections!

Real World

A Faulty Use of Detail answer choice is like a politician who evades a question during a debate:

- Moderator: *Candidate X, what will you do to improve the economy?*
- Candidate X: *You know, that's a wonderful question. My platform is to stand for all Americans' rights and to represent them fairly. If elected, I will help lead our country with integrity.*

True as the claim may be, the response just doesn't answer the question posed!

Bridge

The answers to many *Reasoning Within the Text* questions will be claims unstated by the passage that can nonetheless be inferred. Remember that inferences include assumptions (unstated evidence) and implications (unstated conclusions). Inferences are discussed in Chapter 5 of *MCAT CARS Review*.

as will be the case with the correct answers to many *Reasoning Within the Text* questions, so don't be too quick to reject a choice as OS just because the author does not explicitly say it.

OPPOSITE

Whenever an answer choice contains information that directly conflicts with the passage, we call it an Opposite. Often the difference is due simply to the presence (or absence) of a single word like *not* or *except*, a prefix like *un–* or *a–*, or even a suffix like *–less* or *–free*. Be especially careful when stems or choices involve double (or triple) negatives; they're much less difficult to assess if you reword them with fewer negations. Moreover, don't assume that just because two answer choices contradict each other, that one of them has to be correct. For example, suppose an author argues that it is impossible to prove whether or not a divine being exists, a variant of the religious view known as agnosticism. If a question accompanying the passage were to ask for a claim the author agreed with, *God exists* and *There is no God* would both be Opposites of the correct answer.

DISTORTION

Extreme answers and others that "twist" the ideas in the passage further than the author would prefer are what we call Distortions. Although they do not automatically make a choice incorrect, the following are common signals of distorted claims:

- Strong words like *all*, *always*, *none*, *never*, *impossible*, or *only*
- A prefix like *any–* or *every–*
- A suffix like *–est* or *–less*

MCAT authors typically do not take radical positions on issues, so it's worth noting whenever they do. In those rare cases, extreme choices would not actually be Distortions of the author's view and might be correct. The other major case in which extreme answer choices should not be immediately ruled out is when the question stem tells you that you can treat the answer choices as true and your task is only to gauge which would have the greatest impact on a particular argument. This is often the case with Strengthen–Weaken (Beyond the Passage) questions.

8.3 Signs of a Healthy Answer

If you're like most students prepping for the CARS section, you've had a dispute with at least one question explanation. *Hey, what about what the author says in the first paragraph?* you may have wondered, or perhaps you've said to yourself (or aloud!) *But couldn't you think of it like this instead?* While you may be in the habit of arguing for points with college professors, it does you no good to try to argue with the MCAT. The testmakers are extremely deliberate about how they word correct answers, always taking care to include exactly one per question.

Correct answer choices can vary widely in appearance, but there are patterns in how they are written as well. If the traps that can lead you astray on Test Day are appropriately called Wrong Answer Pathologies, then these corresponding traits can be thought of as indicators of good health. While the following signs are not enough by themselves to make an answer right, you can generally expect them to correspond to the correct choices in most types of questions.

APPROPRIATE SCOPE

You might say correct answers follow the "Goldilocks principle" when it comes to scope: not too broad, not too specific, but just right. The **scope** defines the limits of the discussion, or the particular aspects of the larger topic that the author really cares about. In your Outline, the Goal that you jotted down should give you an idea of the scope of the passage overall. As a general rule (with one important exception), correct answers to MCAT questions will remain within the scope of the passage, but you can formulate a more precise expectation of what scope the correct answer needs to have by identifying the question's type and task.

Main Idea questions will always have correct answers that match the scope of the entire passage. They will typically include at least one wrong answer that is too focused (Faulty Use of Detail) and at least one that goes outside the passage entirely (Out of Scope). In contrast, Detail and Definition-in-Context questions usually require more refined scopes to identify their correct answer choices. If a clue directs you to a particular portion of the passage, then the correct answer more often than not will have the same scope as the referenced text (or what immediately surrounds it).

The important exception to the rule that answers must remain within the scope of the author's discussion applies to the category of *Reasoning Beyond the Text* questions, addressed in Chapter 11 of *MCAT CARS Review*. As their name suggests, these broaden the scope to new contexts, sometimes appearing to have no connection to the passage whatsoever. Note, however, that some *Reasoning Beyond the Text* questions will present new information in the stem but have answers that stick to the scope of the passage anyway. So be savvy with the answer choices in *Reasoning Beyond the Text* questions: while the correct answer choice will tend to lie slightly outside the scope of the passage, don't automatically rule out an answer choice just because it *happens* to be in scope.

MCAT Expertise

The scope of a text refers to the particular aspects of a topic that the author addresses. Every paragraph in a CARS passage has its own scope, and together you can think of them as constituting the scope of the whole passage. Similarly, each answer choice will have its own scope, which could mimic any part of the author's discussion or depart from the passage entirely. It is essential to note that having the same scope doesn't necessarily mean having identical content. For instance, unstated assumptions in an argument are definitely within the scope of the passage, even though the information they contain is left unsaid by the author.

AUTHOR AGREEMENT

Unless a question stem explicitly asks about an alternative viewpoint or a challenge to the information presented in the passage, a correct answer choice will be consistent with what the author says. This is one reason why considerations of *tone* and *voice* (most clearly reflected by Author keywords) are usually important enough to be worth including in your Passage Outline, as was recommended in Chapter 4 of *MCAT CARS Review*. Generally, a correct answer should not contradict anything that the author says elsewhere in the passage, with the possible exception of sentences that speak in a different voice than the author's (such as quotes or references to others' opinions). In short, if it doesn't sound like something the author would say, you'll most likely want to rule it out.

WEAKER IS USUALLY BETTER

One final consideration is a consequence of the fact that the AAMC tends to select passages by authors who do not take extreme views. You may find one or two passages on Test Day with more radical writers; for them, a stronger claim in the answer choices may actually be a good sign. However, for most of the passages you'll encounter, authors tend to use numerous Moderating keywords to limit the strength of their claims. Because a stronger claim has a higher burden of proof (that is, stronger evidence must be provided to support the claim), most authors avoid them to make what they write seem more plausible. Thus, you should generally give preference to answer choices that use weaker language such as *can*, *could*, *may*, *might*, *is possible*, *sometimes*, *often*, *likely*, *probably*, and *in some sense*. Exceptions to this tendency were addressed above in the discussion of Distortion.

Conclusion

This chapter is only an introduction to the question method; the three chapters that follow are a necessary supplement for seeing how the method functions in practice. Specific strategy suggestions and worked examples are included for each of the most common question types and tasks, together constituting well more than 90 percent of what you'll encounter on Test Day. The explanations accompanying these sample questions will also identify their Wrong Answer Pathologies, giving you some concrete examples to go with the explanations provided here.

CONCEPT AND STRATEGY SUMMARY

Kaplan Method for CARS Questions

- Assess
  - Read the question, **NOT** the answers
  - Identify the question type and difficulty
  - Decide to attack *now* or *later*
- Plan
  - Establish the task set by the question type
  - Find clues in the stem on where to research
  - Navigate the passage using your Outline
- Execute
  - Predict what you can about the answer
  - Set expectations for wrong choices
  - Be flexible if your first Plan flops
- Answer
  - Find a match for your prediction, or
  - Eliminate the three wrong options, or
  - Make an educated guess

Wrong Answer Pathologies

- **Faulty Use of Detail (FUD)** answer choices may be accurate statements, but they fail to answer the question posed.
  - The answer choice may be too specific for a question that requires a general answer.
  - The answer choice may use a detail from the wrong part of the passage.
  - The answer choice may be from the right paragraph but still not be relevant to the question posed.
- **Out of Scope (OS)** answer choices usually bring in some element that the passage does not discuss (and that cannot be inferred from the passage).
  - The answer choice may make connections or comparisons that the author did not discuss.
  - The answer choice may make a statement about the significance or history of an idea that the author did not.
  - The answer choice may otherwise bring in information that does not fall within to the constraints of the passage.

- **Opposite** answer choices contain information that directly conflicts with the passage.
  - The answer choice may contain (or omit) a single word like *not* or *except*.
  - The answer choice may contain a prefix like *un–* or *a–* or a suffix like *–less* or *–free*.
  - The answer choice may say that a given claim is true, when the author is ambivalent.
- **Distortion** answer choices are extreme or twist the ideas in the passage further than the author would prefer.
  - The answer choice may use a strong word like *all*, *always*, *none*, *never*, *impossible*, or *only*.
  - The answer choice may contain a prefix like *any–* or *every–* or a suffix like *–est* or *–less*.
  - The answer choice is usually more radical than the author because radical positions are hard to support and are rare in MCAT passages.

Signs of a Healthy Answer

- Correct answers tend to have the right **scope**—not too broad, not too specific, but just right.
- Correct answers tend to be consistent with the author's statements and opinions.
- Correct answers tend to use Moderating keywords, such as *can*, *could*, *may*, *might*, *is possible*, *sometimes*, *often*, *likely*, *probably*, and *in some sense*.

Question Types I: *Foundations of Comprehension Questions*

In This Chapter

Introduction

In order to get into college, you likely had to take an exam like the SAT® or ACT®, both of which feature sections that test reading comprehension. Most of the questions in these sections were straightforward, requiring you merely to search the text for a key fact, to define the meaning of a term used in a passage, or to identify the author's thesis. Some of the more challenging questions may have required you to understand what the author was *doing* with a part of the passage, to imagine things from the writer's perspective, or to explain why she used a certain word or phrase. Such questions can also be found in the *Critical Analysis and Reasoning Skills* (CARS) section of the MCAT. However, these will constitute only 30 percent of the questions you encounter on Test Day, and they will take more difficult forms than you saw on those precollege exams. Our research of all of the released MCAT material indicates that Detail questions make up about half of the *Foundations of Comprehension* questions, or about eight or nine questions. The other question types in this category show up in about two or three questions each.

This chapter and the next two will follow the same general pattern. For each question type, we will briefly discuss what makes that type distinctive before examining some sample question stems. Then, after discussing strategy, we'll revisit one of the passages first introduced in Chapter 7 of *MCAT CARS Review*, providing at least one sample question of each type. The question types in this chapter all fall under the *Foundations of Comprehension* category and will be examined in this order: Main Idea, Detail, Function, and Definition-in-Context.

Note: The Question Types, as well as the Kaplan Method for CARS Passages, Kaplan Method for CARS Questions, and Wrong Answer Pathologies are included as tear-out sheets in the back of this book.

9.1 Main Idea Questions

Questions that ask about the big picture of the passage are what we call **Main Idea questions**. Only about 5 percent of the questions in the CARS section fall into this type, but they are easy to recognize and the Kaplan Method for CARS Passages arms you with everything you need to attack them.

SAMPLE QUESTION STEMS

- The author's central thesis is that:
- Which of the following best characterizes the main idea of the passage?
- The primary purpose of the passage is to:
- The author of the passage is primarily interested in:
- Which of the following titles best captures the main theme of the passage?
- The author can best be viewed as a proponent of:
- The language used in the passage makes it clear that the intended audience is:
- What is the author's central concern?

Main Idea questions will either use some variant of the phrase *central thesis*, *primary purpose*, or—of course—*main idea*, or else make some kind of general reference to *the author*. On rare occasions, Main Idea questions will bring in a more challenging aspect of the rhetorical situation, such as the *audience* or the *medium*.

STRATEGY

Decide to do a Main Idea question as soon as you encounter it because these questions can gain you some quick points. Your best bet for a Plan is simply to *Go for the Goal!* In fact, this is one of the reasons it's worth Reflecting on the passage at the end of your reading: the Goal that you write down in your outline gives you an instant prediction for questions of this type. Note that the verb you choose will often be as important a part of your prediction as any of the words that follow.

In the event that none of the choices come close to matching what you thought the author's Goal was, use process of elimination to remove Faulty Uses of Detail that are too narrow, Out of Scope options that go too far afield, and any choice that has the wrong tone (positive, negative, ambivalent, or impartial) or degree (extreme *vs.* moderate).

WORKED EXAMPLE—A PSYCHOLOGY PASSAGE

There is no shortage of evidence for the existence of systemic biases in ordinary human reasoning. For instance, Kahneman and Tversky in their groundbreaking 1974 work proposed the existence of a heuristic—an error-prone shortcut in reasoning—known as "anchoring." In one of their most notable experiments, participants were exposed to the spin of a roulette wheel (specially rigged to land randomly on one of only two possible results) before being asked to guess what percent of United Nations member states were African. The half of the sample who had the roulette wheel stop at 65 guessed, on average, that 45% of the UN was African, while those with a result of 10 guessed only 25%, demonstrating that prior presentation of a random number otherwise unconnected to a quantitative judgment can still influence that judgment.

The anchoring effect has been observed on repeated other occasions, such as in Dan Ariely's experiment that used digits in Social Security numbers as an anchor for bids at an auction, and in the 1996 study by Wilson et al. that showed even awareness of the existence of anchoring bias is insufficient to mitigate its effects. The advertising industry has long been aware of this bias, the rationale for its frequent practice of featuring an "original" price before showing a "sale" price that is invariably reduced. Of course, anchoring is hardly alone among the defective tendencies in human reasoning; other systemic biases have also been experimentally identified, including loss aversion, the availability heuristic, and optimism bias.

Example:

1. The author's primary task in the passage is to:
   A. search for evidence of systematic biases in normal human thinking.
   B. discuss empirical findings on anchoring and other reasoning biases.
   C. show that anchoring is the most commonly occurring error in reasoning.
   D. demonstrate that knowledge of anchoring bias is insufficient to prevent it.

Solution: The phrase *primary task* tells you that this is a Main Idea question, so let's look again at the outline we generated for this brief passage in Chapter 7 of *MCAT CARS Review*:

P1. Systemic biases in reasoning: ex. anchoring heuristic (evidence: Kahneman & Tversky)

P2. More evidence for anchoring (Ariely, Wilson et al.); other systemic biases

Goal: To present evidence for systemic biases in reasoning, especially anchoring

Using that Goal, or the Goal you generated during your own Outline attempt, your prediction should immediately lead you to **choice (B)**. The phrase *discuss empirical findings* is roughly equivalent in meaning to our *present evidence*. Also, the scope is right, with the answer focusing on anchoring first but mentioning other biases as well because the author does introduce anchoring as an example with the phrase *For instance*.

On Test Day, whenever you find an easy match for a prediction that you made, a choice that fulfills your expectation for correctness, go with that Answer and move on to Assess the next question. But for these examples, it's worth discussing what goes wrong in the other options. **Choice (A)** comes close and has the appropriate scope, but the verb is wrong: in the very first sentence, the author says that *There is no shortage of evidence*, so why would the author's task be to *search for* something so readily available? Moving on to **choice (C)**, we find an Out of Scope choice: while the author says that systematic biases are common to thinking, there is never any comparison among the types mentioned. Just because the author focuses on anchoring does *not* mean that anchoring is necessarily the most frequently occurring—the author could choose to discuss it for any number of reasons other than its commonness. Finally, **choice (D)** is a Faulty Use of Detail because it is too specific. The referenced claim is made in the second paragraph, but it applies only to the study conducted by Wilson and others. This answer does not encompass the focus of the whole passage.

9.2 Detail Questions

Detail questions ask about what is stated explicitly in the passage. These are probably what you typically think of when you imagine a "reading comprehension" question because they tend to require searching the text to fill in the missing piece. While Main Idea questions focus on the big picture, Detail questions zoom in on some of the finer points of the passage. They are by far the most common type of the *Foundations of Comprehension* category, constituting at least half of the questions that fall under this heading.

SAMPLE QUESTION STEMS

- According to the author's account of [topic], [concept] is:
- The author states that [person] holds the view that:
- Which of the following, according to the passage, does the author associate with the idea of [concept]?

MCAT Expertise

According to our research of released AAMC material, Detail questions make up about 16 percent of the CARS section (about eight or nine questions).

- The author's apparent attitude toward [alternative position] is:
- Based on the discussion in [paragraph reference], the work of [artist/writer] was widely regarded as:
- The passage suggests which of the following about [topic]? [List of Roman numerals]
- The author asserts all of the following EXCEPT:
- Which of the following claims does NOT appear in the passage?

Detail questions tend to contain simple, declarative language (*is* and *are*) rather than the subjunctive mood (*would* and *could*), often include phrases like *the author states* and *according to the passage*, and more often than not take the form of incomplete sentences ending with a colon.

The last three examples listed fall into what is known as the Scattered subtype. A **Scattered** question is one that either employs a set of Roman numeral options or uses a word like EXCEPT, NOT, or LEAST. While just about any type of question can be Scattered—from Scattered Function to Scattered Inference—Scattered Detail is perhaps the most popular instance of the Scattered subtype.

STRATEGY

The only trick to working with Detail questions is that sometimes a seemingly straightforward question can actually require making an inference. If you are dealing with a true Detail question, though, your Plan should be to follow the clues in the question stem, especially the content **buzzwords**, looking to your Outline to help you home in on the relevant portion of the passage. Once you find the precise sentence referenced, remember to read at least the sentence before and the sentence after (unless of course you're looking at the first or last sentence of the entire passage!) to get a bit more context. Once you've read the relevant text, create your prediction by putting the sentence in your own words, and then look for the best match to Answer the question..

You will likely want to save the Scattered Detail questions you encounter for later because these will often require researching three or four different parts of the text, rather than just one. When working with these questions, your outline will prove extremely useful for locating everything you need to find. Process of elimination is almost inevitable with questions of the Scattered subtype, but that doesn't mean you should immediately jump to the answer choices. As with any question, take what you can from the stem to set some basic expectations. You have your Outline, as well as the experience you will have gained working on other questions in the set, to help with this. If you come across a choice that you know the passage does not contain, then go with it as the correct answer.

Bridge

Sometimes, what appears to be a Detail question will actually require you to make an inference. Inference questions include both Assumption and Implication questions, the strategies for which are discussed in Chapter 10 of *MCAT CARS Review*.

MCAT Expertise

For Detail questions, make sure to paraphrase the relevant text in a "short and sweet" format that will be easy to repeat to yourself while reading the answer choices. Much of the challenge of this type of question can be trying to figure out which answer choice actually matches your prediction—so make your prediction something that's easy to remember!

WORKED EXAMPLES—AN ARTS PASSAGE

One of the first examples of the ascendance of abstraction in 20th-century art is the Dada movement, which Lowenthal dubbed "the groundwork to abstract art and sound poetry, a starting point for performance art, a prelude to postmodernism, an influence on pop art … and the movement that laid the foundation for surrealism." Dadaism was ultimately premised on a philosophical rejection of the dominant culture, which is to say the dominating culture of colonialist Europe. Not content with the violent exploitation of other peoples, the gaze of Europe's ruling factions once again turned inward, reigniting provincial disputes into the conflagration that came to be known by the Eurocentric epithet "World War I"—the European subcontinent apparently being the only part of the world that mattered.

The absurd destructiveness of the Great War was a natural prelude to the creative absurdity of Dada. Is it any wonder that the rejection of reason made manifest by senseless atrocities should lead to the embrace of irrationality and disorder among the West's subaltern artistic communities? Marcel Janco, one of the first Dadaists, cited this rationale: "We had lost confidence in our culture. Everything had to be demolished. We would begin again after the *tabula rasa*." Thus, we find the overturning of what was once considered art: a urinal becomes the *Fountain* after Marcel Duchamp signs it "R. Mutt" in 1917, the nonsense syllables of Hugo Ball and Kurt Schwitters transform into "sound poems," dancers in cardboard cubist costumes accompanied by foghorns and typewriters metamorphosize into the ballet *Parade*. Unsurprisingly, many commentators, including founding members, have described Dada as an "anti-art" movement. Notwithstanding such a designation, Dadaism has left a lasting imprint on modern Western art.

Example:

2. As stated in the passage, prior to the Great War, the leaders of Europe were primarily focused on:
   A. fighting one another in World War I.
   B. colonizing other parts of the globe.
   C. gazing inward at local problems.
   D. rejecting the dominant culture.

Solution: When the stem says *as stated in the passage*, it usually signifies a Detail question (with some exceptions noted in the next chapter). You'll most likely want to work on it right away. There are two buzzwords in the question stem: *the Great War* and *the leaders of Europe*. The first comes directly from the start of paragraph 2, where you can judge from the context that it must be another name for what we now call World War I. (They of course didn't know there was going to be a second one at the time!) The second buzzword does not appear exactly, but it shows up in the synonymous phrase *Europe's ruling factions* in the last sentence of paragraph 1. In addition to reading these two sentences, it may be worth reading one before and one after.

In fact, the preceding sentence offers a key bit of context, illustrating that the author regards European culture quite negatively, with the phrase *the dominating culture of colonialist Europe*. More of the same follows with the phrase *violent exploitation of other peoples*, as this author highlights Europe's past as a global colonizer. The phrase *gaze … once again turned inward* is noteworthy for mirroring the optical language of *focused on* featured in the question stem. Putting this all together sets a thorough expectation for the correct answer: if the turning inward happened with the Great War, then prior to that, Europe's leaders must have been looking outward, focusing on their colonial acquisitions. This prediction finds a perfect match in **choice (B)**.

Among the wrong options, **choice (A)** is based on a misunderstanding of the terminology. Though World War I is mentioned in the prior sentence, the author calls attention to the fact that it only later came to be known by that epithet (name), then in the following sentence uses another name for it. Because the two terms refer to the same event, European leaders could not be focused on it before it happened. In contrast, **choice (C)** is an Opposite because Europeans were actually gazing outward at their colonies. Finally, **choice (D)** is a Faulty Use of Detail: that phrase appears almost exactly, but it actually describes the founders of the Dada movement, not the European leaders.

Example:

3. Based on the passage, which of the following is not a characteristic associated with Dadaism?

A. A renunciation of European culture

B. A reputation as an "anti-art" movement

C. Importance for later 20th-century art

D. The embrace of irrational atrocities

Solution: Although the testmaker will often put the word *not* in italics or all caps, sometimes it will appear plainly in a question stem, as seen here. Don't be fooled: this is still a Scattered Detail question. Because Scattered Detail questions are often time-consuming, you'd likely want to make it the last question you work on in the question set. That said, don't forget to make a Plan and set some basic expectations. The phrasing *a characteristic associated with* is vague enough that it could mean something the author says or potentially another view identified in the passage. That means you can't rule out an answer choice just because it doesn't sound like something the author would say, so long as it sounds like something someone else in the passage would. Because both paragraphs are chock-full of claims about Dadaism, there's no point in searching the text to set additional expectations—you'll have to go with this more minimal Plan.

Choice (A) comes directly from the author's second sentence: *Dadaism was ultimately premised on a philosophical rejection of the ... culture of colonialist Europe.* The word *renunciation* is a synonym of *rejection*—so cross off this option. Moving on to the next choice, while the author explicitly rejected the idea that Dadaism is "anti-art," that view is still reflected in the passage in the next-to-last sentence, where the author writes *many commentators, including founding members, have described Dada as an "anti-art" movement.* Another way of saying that many commentators describe it that way is to say that is has a reputation. Hence, **choice (B)** should also be eliminated. The next characteristic is found at both the beginning of the passage, with the quotation from Lowenthal, and at the end, with the author's statement that *Dadaism has left a lasting imprint on modern Western art.* With **choice (C)** now off the table, we know that **choice (D)** must be the answer—but let's talk about it anyway.

This choice is very close to being a characteristic; however, the word *atrocities* prevents it from being associated with Dadaism and makes it the correct choice. The key sentence is worth repeating in full in order to untangle it: *Is it any wonder that the rejection of reason made manifest by senseless atrocities should lead to the embrace of irrationality and disorder among the West's subaltern artistic communities?* The author is saying that Dadaism embraces irrationality, although not in the same way that irrationality (*rejection of reason*) manifests itself in warfare (*senseless atrocities*). The preceding sentence offers some useful clarification: *The absurd destructiveness of the Great War was a natural prelude to the creative absurdity of Dada.* Notice how the word *absurd* is used to join two concepts that are typically viewed as opposites: creation and destruction. The author is suggesting that, even though both the Great War and Dadaism defied reason, they did so in dramatically different ways. This irrationality or absurdness in Dadaism stood in opposition to the atrocities of World War I; the word *embrace* in the answer choice makes this statement *not a characteristic* of Dadaism. That's why **choice (D)** is correct.

9.3 Function Questions

One of the reasons that the Kaplan Method for CARS Passages emphasizes reading for perspective (trying to understand the author's attitude and intentions) is that the entire **Function question** type specifically asks about what the author is trying to *do* in the passage. Unlike a Main Idea question, which might ask about the overall Goal of the passage, a Function question will ask about the purpose of only a portion of it. Function questions are just about as common as Main Idea questions, constituting only about 5 percent of what you'll see in this section on Test Day.

MCAT Expertise

According to our research of released AAMC material, Function questions make up about 5 percent of the CARS section (about two or three questions).

SAMPLE QUESTION STEMS

- What is the author's apparent purpose in stating [quotation]?
- The author mentions [topic] in [paragraph reference] in order to:
- Which of the following is the most probable reason for the author's inclusion of a quotation from [person]?
- The author's reference to [concept] in [paragraph reference] is most likely supposed to show:
- When the author says [claim], she is emphasizing that:
- Which of the following is the example from [paragraph reference] most likely intended to suggest?
- The author compares [one concept] to [another concept] because:
- The author's principal motive for discussing [alternative position] is to explain that:

What should be readily apparent in the phrasing of Function questions is frequent mention of the author and the use of direct references to the text—especially through paragraph references. Language like *purpose*, *motive*, and *intention* indicate a Function question, as do phrases that end with *in order to* and *because*.

STRATEGY

The Outline will be key when working with a Function question. If you were reading for perspective by looking out for Author keywords (which give a glimpse inside the author's point of view), you may have already included the information you need to answer such a question in your Outline. Keep in mind that, generally speaking, Function questions work in a nested way. In other words, the passage as a whole has a purpose, and each paragraph within it has a subordinate function that is distinctive but that contributes to the larger whole. Each paragraph can in turn be broken down into sentences, each of which has its own particular role to play in the paragraph—and even sentences can be broken down to particular words or phrases.

Key Concept

Both Main Idea and Function questions can often be answered solely by looking at your Passage Outline. The answers to Main Idea questions should reflect the author's Goal, whereas the answers to Function questions should usually reflect the Label you've assigned to a given paragraph.

Because a Function question will generally ask for the purpose of no more than a paragraph, to formulate some initial expectations, you should go to your Outline and look at the Label for the specific paragraph and perhaps also look at the Goal. Then, if buzzwords in the question stem direct you to specific sentences, reread those portions of the paragraph and think about how it fits into both the purpose of the paragraph and the passage's general Goal. Formulate a statement of what the desired function is, and then start to look for an Answer that matches.

Remember that if you can't find a perfect match, you can eliminate choices that would be inconsistent with functions at a higher level. So, for example, the purpose of a paragraph will not be at odds with the author's Goal for the passage as a whole. Even when authors bring up information that conflicts with their main arguments, they commonly do so for the sake of shooting it down—answering or countering a refutation, as discussed in Chapter 5 of *MCAT CARS Review*.

WORKED EXAMPLE—AN ETHICS PASSAGE

The most prevalent argument against doctor-assisted suicide relies upon a distinction between *passive* and *active* euthanasia—in essence, the difference between killing someone and letting that person die. On this account, a physician is restricted by her Hippocratic oath to do no harm and thus cannot act in ways that would inflict the ultimate harm, death. In contrast, failing to resuscitate an individual who is dying is permitted because this would only be an instance of refraining from help and not a willful cause of harm. The common objection to this distinction, that it is vague and therefore difficult to apply, does not carry much weight. After all, applying ethical principles of *any sort* to the complexities of the world is an enterprise fraught with imprecision.

Rather, the fundamental problem with the distinction is that it is not an ethically relevant one, readily apparent in the following thought experiment. Imagine a terminally ill patient hooked up to an unusual sort of life support device, one that only functioned to prevent a separate "suicide machine" from administering a lethal injection so long as the doctor pressed a button on it once per day. Would there be any relevant difference between using the suicide machine directly and not using the prevention device? The intention of the doctor would be the same (fulfilling the patient's wish to die), and the effect would be the same (an injection causing the patient's death). The only variance here is the means by which the effect comes about, and this is not an ethical difference but merely a technical one.

Example:

4. The author's apparent intention in discussing the "suicide machine" in paragraph 2 is to:

    A. support his thesis using an imaginative exercise.

    B. question the idea that vagueness is ethically relevant.

    C. explain the operation of a piece of medical equipment.

    D. propose a new method for performing euthanasia.

Solution: As with the Main Idea example above, looking at our Outline for this passage from Chapter 7 of *MCAT CARS Review* will make this question much more manageable:

P1. "Most prevalent argument" against euthanasia assumes passive/active difference (vague is okay)

P2. Author: distinction is not ethically relevant (supported w/ thought experiment)

Goal: To argue the distinction between passive and active euthanasia is not ethically relevant

The purpose listed for paragraph 2 even includes a note about the "suicide machine" thought experiment's role as support, so this will suffice as a prediction. Going back to the text shouldn't be necessary unless the answer choices take us somewhere that we completely didn't expect. Fortunately, this is not the case with this question, and we can see that **choice (A)** gives us precisely what we need. That time spent Outlining has been more than paid back with a quick correct response.

Among the wrong answers, **choice (B)** is wrong for bringing in *vagueness*, when the point of the thought experiment is more to question whether the *passive/active distinction* is ethically relevant—not vagueness. **Choice (C)** might be considered a Faulty Use of Detail because the operation of this machine is explained. However, the machine is being described not for its own sake—it's imaginary, after all—but simply to illustrate a point. The final incorrect option, **choice (D)**, would be a product of taking the thought experiment too literally.

9.4 Definition-in-Context Questions

Definition-in-Context questions constitute the final type that falls into the *Foundations of Comprehension* category. The task involved with such questions is always the same: define the word or phrase, specifically as it is used in the passage. You can expect to see two or three of them on Test Day, as they tend to make up about 4 percent of all questions in the CARS section.

MCAT Expertise

According to our research of released AAMC material, Definition-in-Context questions make up about 4 percent of the CARS section (about two questions).

SAMPLE QUESTION STEMS

- As used by the author, the word [term] most nearly means:
- In [paragraph reference], what is the author's most likely meaning when stating [quotation]?
- The author's choice of the phrase [term] is probably intended to suggest:
- As used in the passage, [term] refers to:
- In [paragraph reference], the author asserts that [claim]. What the author most likely means by this is:
- Which of the following is most synonymous with [concept] as discussed in the text?

This list of stems makes it clear that Definition-in-Context questions always feature a reference to a word, phrase, or an entire claim from the passage, the meaning of which you are tasked with identifying. Quotation marks and italics are common features used to call attention to the terms, but on occasion a Definition-in-Context question stem may lack these.

STRATEGY

Although these questions ask about the meanings of words, a dictionary will not help you here, and in some cases it could even lead you astray. Trap answers in these questions are often the common definitions of the word, which are tempting Out of Scope choices that fail to match the context. That said, these questions tend to be relatively quick because they refer only to small portions of the text. Thus, you should generally decide to work on these questions as soon as you see them.

Your Plan with a Definition-in-Context question will be to go to the text and surrounding context, if necessary, to see how the word or phrase is actually used in the passage. With this question type, the question stems will usually contain a paragraph reference, but use your Outline if necessary to locate the relevant sentence. If reading that sentence doesn't give you enough to work with, then look at the one before and after. Then phrase a definition in your own words, based on what you see. Author keywords may be especially helpful because answer choices with the wrong tone can immediately be ruled out.

MCAT Expertise

An author may imbue common words with a special meaning in the passage. Therefore, make sure to check how the author actually uses the word in a Definition-in-Context question, rather than looking for a dictionary definition of the term. Wrong answers in these questions are often accurate definitions of the term that do not match how the term was used in the passage.

WORKED EXAMPLE—A HISTORY PASSAGE

In 1941, an exuberant nationalist wrote: "We must accept wholeheartedly our duty and our opportunity as the most powerful and vital nation … to exert upon the world the full impact of our influence, for such purposes as we see fit and by such means as we see fit." If forced to guess the identity of the writer, many US citizens would likely suspect a German jingoist advocating for *Lebensraum*. In actuality, the sentiment was expressed by one of America's own: Henry Luce, the highly influential publisher of the magazines *Life*, *Time*, and *Fortune*. Luce sought to dub the 1900s the "American Century," calling upon the nation to pursue global hegemony as it slipped from the grasp of warring Old World empires. As a forecast of world history, Luce's pronouncement seems prescient—but is it justifiable as a normative stance?

Not all of Luce's contemporaries bought into his exceptionalist creed. Only a year later, Henry Wallace, vice president under FDR, insisted that no country had the "right to exploit other nations" and that "military [and] economic imperialism" were invariably immoral. It is a foundational assumption in ethics that the wrongness of an act is independent of the particular identity of the actor—individuals who pay no heed to moral consistency are justly condemned as hypocrites. So why should it be any different for nation-states? In accord with this principle, Wallace proselytized for "the century of the common man," for the furtherance of a "great revolution of the people," and for bringing justice and prosperity to all persons irrespective of accidents of birth. Sadly, Wallace never had the chance to lead the United States in this cosmopolitan direction; prior to Roosevelt's demise at the beginning of his fourth term, the vice presidency was handed to Harry Truman, a man whose narrow provincialism ensconced him firmly in Luce's camp. And with Truman came the ghastly atomic eradication of two Japanese cities, the dangerous precedent set by military action without congressional approval in Korea, and a Cold War with the Soviet Union that brought the world to the brink of nuclear destruction.

Example:

5. The author's use of the term provincialism in paragraph 2 comes closest in meaning to:

   A. German jingoism.

   B. economic imperialism.

   C. nationalistic exceptionalism.

   D. exuberant cosmopolitanism.

Solution: The clue in the question stem points to the second paragraph, but the reference might still be difficult to find in a paragraph full of –*ism*s. The key sentence is this: *Sadly, Wallace never had the chance to lead the United States in this cosmopolitan direction; prior to Roosevelt's demise at the beginning of his fourth term, the vice presidency was handed to Harry Truman, a man whose narrow provincialism ensconced him firmly in Luce's camp.* This sentence gives you a lot to work with. You can see that *provincialism* is a view attributed to Truman and Luce, who are contraposed to the *cosmopolitan* Wallace. In a passage that features a few different perspectives, it's not surprising to see a question like this that requires keeping straight who holds which view. This passage presents two major sides, and it's clear that *provincialism* represents a view that belongs to Truman, whose views align with those of Luce.

With these expectations established, look for a match in the answers. Because both nationalism (at the start of paragraph 1) and exceptionalism (at the start of paragraph 2) are views attributed to Luce, it is evident that **choice (C)** must be correct. **Choice (A)** is a Faulty Use of Detail; *a German jingoist* was mentioned in the first paragraph, but this is no good because Luce and Truman are both Americans. **Choice (B)** echoes the quote from Wallace as he criticizes Luce—*"military [and] economic imperialism"*—but all of the examples given for Truman show evidence of military action, not economic: *the ghastly atomic eradication of two Japanese cities, the dangerous precedent set by military action without congressional approval in Korea, and a Cold War with the Soviet Union that brought the world to the brink of nuclear destruction.* The emphasis in **choice (B)** is therefore displaced. Lastly, **choice (D)** uses a variant of *cosmopolitan*, a characteristic that was attributed to Wallace, so it's an Opposite.

Conclusion

Reading comprehension is a skill you've honed through your whole life—most exams you've had in literature and English classes have most likely centered on your ability to understand the text you read. On the MCAT, reading comprehension is important not only for answering *Foundations of Comprehension* questions but also for understanding the passage itself. While they take many forms, including Main Idea, Detail, Function, and Definition-in-Context questions, all *Foundations of Comprehension* questions share a few common features. Answering all of these question types is facilitated by a well-constructed Outline, which can be used to locate the relevant text for the answer or—in the case of Main Idea questions—will contain the answer itself. Also, the answers to all of these questions must be stated or paraphrased directly in the passage. These question types also differ in significant ways. For example, Main Idea and Definition-in-Context questions should usually be answered as soon as you see them, whereas Detail (especially Scattered Detail) questions may be more time-consuming and should therefore be saved until the end of the question set. Each question type has a specific Plan, as described in this chapter. We'll continue discussing question types in the next two chapters, as we explore *Reasoning Within the Text* and *Reasoning Beyond the Text* questions.

CONCEPT AND STRATEGY SUMMARY

Main Idea Questions

- Assess: **Main Idea questions** ask for the author's primary Goal.

  - These questions often contain words like *central thesis*, *primary purpose*, or *main idea*.

  - Less commonly, these questions may ask about a different aspect of the rhetorical situation such as the *audience* or the *medium*.

- Plan: Look at what you wrote in your Outline for the Goal.

- Execute: Reread the Goal in your Outline, taking note of the charge and degree of the verb (positive *vs.* negative, extreme *vs.* moderate).

- Answer: Match your expectations with the right answer. If there is no clear match, or if you cannot perform any of the earlier steps of the Kaplan Method for CARS Questions, use process of elimination.

  - Wrong answer choices may be too narrow (Faulty Use of Detail) or too broad (Out of Scope).

  - Wrong answer choices may have the wrong tone (positive, negative, ambivalent, or impartial) or degree (too extreme or too moderate).

Detail Questions

- Assess: **Detail questions** ask about what is stated explicitly in the passage.

  - These questions tend to use words like *the author states* or *according to the passage*, with declarative language like *is* and *are*.

  - Detail questions are the most likely to use the **Scattered** format, which uses Roman numeral options or words like *EXCEPT*, *NOT*, or *LEAST*.

- Plan: Look for content buzzwords in the question stem and check your Outline to determine where the relevant information will be found.

- Execute: Reread the relevant sentence, as well as the sentences before and after. Create your prediction by putting the answer in your own words.

  - Make the prediction brief so you can repeat it to yourself between answer choices.

  - For Scattered Detail questions, locate all three of the wrong answers in the passage so you can eliminate them from the options.

- Answer: Match your expectations with the right answer. If there is no clear match, or if you cannot perform any of the earlier steps of the Kaplan Method for CARS Questions, use process of elimination.

Function Questions

- Assess: **Function questions** ask about what the author is trying to *do* during the passage.
    - ○ These questions are similar to Main Idea questions, although they focus on the purpose of only one portion of the passage (usually one sentence or one paragraph).
    - ○ Function questions tend to use words like *purpose*, *motive*, or *intention* or phrases like *in order to* or *because*.
- Plan: Use your Outline to locate the relevant paragraph.
- Execute: Look at your Label for the relevant paragraph and the Goal at the bottom of your Outline. If buzzwords in the question stem direct you to specific sentences, reread those portions, thinking about how they fit into the purpose of the paragraph and the overall passage.
- Answer: Match your expectations with the right answer. If there is no clear match, or if you cannot perform any of the earlier steps of the Kaplan Method for CARS Questions, use process of elimination, removing any answer that conflicts with the author's main argument or the paragraph's purpose.

Definition-in-Context Questions

- Assess: **Definition-in-Context questions** ask you to define a word or phrase as it is used in the passage.
    - ○ These questions often call attention to the term to be defined using quotation marks or italics, but not always.
    - ○ Definition-in-Context questions always reference a word, phrase, or an entire claim from the passage.
- Plan: Use your Outline to locate the relevant paragraph.
- Execute: Reread the sentence with the word or phrase, and perhaps the surrounding context. Rephrase the author's definition of the term in your own words.
- Answer: Match your expectations with the right answer. If there is no clear match, or if you cannot perform any of the earlier steps of the Kaplan Method for CARS Questions, use process of elimination.

Question Types II:
Reasoning Within the Text Questions

In This Chapter

Introduction

How many times have you been told that *you should never assume*? Whether you were simply told that assumptions breed mistakes or given some more colorful rationale, this generally sound advice can only go so far. In reality, it is impossible *not* to make assumptions because an assumption is just anything that we take for granted—that we believe without additional evidence. It simply does not matter how rational or scientifically curious you consider yourself to be: at some point you stop asking *Why?* and start to take things on faith. Authors of passages used in *Critical Analysis and Reasoning Skills* (CARS) are of course no different, and the Association of American Medical Colleges (AAMC) will test that you can identify the assumptions that they hold, as well as the other essential elements of the reasoning they employ in their passages.

In this chapter, we'll continue the treatment of question types first employed with *Foundations of Comprehension*, now examining the two types of *Reasoning Within the Text* questions that Kaplan has identified: Inference questions, which ask about the implied parts of arguments, and Strengthen–Weaken (Within the Passage) questions, which predominantly concern the ways in which arguments are backed by evidence and undermined by refutations. We adopt the same general approach as before: after identifying what makes the questions distinctive and offering several common question stems, we discuss strategies for the tasks each type involves, illustrating them with a few worked examples.

Reasoning Within the Text questions account for 30 percent of what you'll encounter on Test Day, according to both the AAMC's official statements and Kaplan's own extensive research of released AAMC material. Our data indicate that a bit more than half fall into the Inference category, so this type will account for approximately one-sixth of the CARS section or about eight or nine questions. This means Inference questions are roughly as common as Detail and Strengthen–Weaken (Beyond the Passage) questions, but they are less common than Apply questions. Strengthen–Weaken (Within the Passage) questions are slightly rarer, averaging about six questions per section.

Note: The question types, as well as the Kaplan Method for CARS Passages, Kaplan Method for CARS Questions, and Wrong Answer Pathologies are included as tear-out sheets in the back of this book.

10.1 Inference Questions

What makes **Inference questions** distinctive is that they deal with unstated parts of arguments: information that is not explicitly written by the author but that *must* be true given what is claimed in the passage. It is crucial to understand that the correct answers to Inference questions are not simply assertions that are *possibly* true or that *could* be accurate; rather, they are necessary assumptions or at least highly probable implications. We call these kinds of questions Inference because, as first noted in Chapter 5 of *MCAT CARS Review*, it is the common name of the process used to arrive at both **assumptions** (unstated evidence) and **implications** (unstated conclusions), collectively known as inferences.

SAMPLE QUESTION STEMS

- In [paragraph reference], it is reasonable to believe that the author assumes:
- Implicit in the discussion of [topic] is the underlying assumption that:
- The passage suggests [claim] because:
- On the basis of the author's account of [topic], which of the following might reasonably be inferred?
- The author implies that [concept] is NOT:
- It is reasonable to conclude that the author regards [person or position] as:
- The author says [quotation], but also [paraphrase of different claim]. These beliefs imply:
- Which of the following inferences is most justified by information provided in the passage? [List of Roman numerals]

As these examples indicate, during the first step of the Kaplan Method for CARS Questions—in which you Assess the question type—you can recognize that you might be dealing with an Inference question if you see one or more of the following

MCAT Expertise

According to our research of released AAMC material, Inference questions make up about 16 percent of the CARS section (about eight or nine questions).

words (or variations of them): *assume*, *because*, *conclude*, *imply*, *infer*, *justify*, *reasonable*, and *suggest*. However, if a question stem contains any of these words and new information of some kind, then it will fall into the *Reasoning Beyond the Text* category instead. If there are no new elements, you are likely dealing with an Inference question.

There is actually something of a continuum between Detail and Inference questions; the position of questions on that continuum varies based on the complexity of the reasoning used to solve them. A question that tells you to make an *inference* might require one relatively simple step, such as canceling out a double negative or identifying a paraphrase of lines from the passage. Sometimes you'll even find yourself looking for an item that the *passage suggests* or the *author implies* but, after Executing your Plan, discover that the answer was in the text virtually word for word. In cases such as these, consider yourself fortunate because you've uncovered a Detail question in disguise! The predictions you make for these questions will likely be more than adequate to reach the correct answer.

The downside to this ambiguity is that sometimes a question that uses simple declarative language will require a lot more critical thinking than it initially seems. Just because a stem includes a phrase like *the author asserts* or *as stated in the passage* (common question stems for Detail questions) does not necessarily mean that the answer is stated straightforwardly. Notwithstanding such trickery on the part of the AAMC, as long as you recognize the possibility that apparent Detail questions can be disguised Inference questions and are prepared to apply the Denial Test strategy to those questions, you can avoid being fooled!

STRATEGY

There are only two basic tasks with the Inference question type. When you recognize that you need to make an inference, first ask yourself whether you are looking for a missing but essential piece of evidence (an **assumption**) or for a conclusion that is unstated but highly probable given what is said (an **implication**).

Assumptions

If your task is to identify an assumption, the first prong of your attack Plan should be to determine what claim it is supposed to underlie. Sometimes the question stem will say this explicitly, or it may use quoted text or paragraph numbers to refer to a particular claim. Use your Outline if necessary to find the relevant sentences from the passage. When you Execute your Plan, reread those sentences and isolate the specific statement, taking care to see whether there's any existing evidence in the surrounding text that's used to support it. Logic keywords are your best friends here, but keep in mind that a lot of authors use them sparsely, so

Key Concept

Inferences are unstated parts of arguments that must be true based on what the passage says. Assumptions are unstated pieces of evidence, while implications are unstated conclusions.

they won't always be there to help. The Answer to assumption questions might include words or ideas that are similar to a piece of evidence actually stated, so you can use any that you locate for your prediction, or just go with whatever links the evidence provided to the conclusion when you reread the text—*now I see what the author is taking for granted!*

Implications

Whenever the task is finding an implication, isolate in the text any particular sentences referred to in the question stem and watch out for Logic keywords, just as with assumptions. Now, however, you'll be looking to see whether the particular statements referenced are used to support anything else. If so, use those explicitly supported conclusions to set your expectations for the correct answer because sometimes implications will be quite similar to them. Alternatively, if another implication occurs to you when you reread, you can use that as a prediction.

Whenever you can't find a match for your prediction—if you at first thought it was a Detail, if you didn't know where to look because the stem had no paragraph reference clues, or if the answer choices just turned out very differently than you expected—Plan B is to use a special version of process of elimination known as the **Denial Test**. Let's take a look at how it works in practice.

The Denial Test

For each answer choice, negate (take the opposite of) what is being said. In question stems that end with colons (:), you may need to take part of the text from the end of the stem and combine it with the answer choice to create a sentence that can then be denied. Be careful with sentences that already contain negative words, prefixes, and suffixes because sometimes just removing that text is not enough to change the meaning in the proper way, as shown in the first worked example on the following page. If nothing else, any claim can be denied by adding *It is not the case that* to the beginning of the sentence. Once you've denied the claim, think about the effect it has on the passage. If you're not sure what effect it has, look for clues in the question stem or the choice itself to see if it references a particular part of the passage that you could reread to get an idea. Don't forget to use your Outline to help navigate. If it's clear that the negated claim has no significant impact, then cross it off.

When you come across an answer choice that logically conflicts with the text once you've negated it, you've likely found your correct answer. However, sometimes multiple answer choices will have denials that cause problems for the text, so when Executing the Denial Test you should *always test every answer choice* and pick the one where negation has the most detrimental impact on arguments or assertions from the passage. Keep in mind that this can be time-consuming, which is why it's generally a good idea to triage the question once you discover no quicker approach will serve.

It is hard to understand how the Denial Test works simply by reading about it. Check out the worked example below and make sure to practice the Denial Test on Inference questions to get used to using it.

WORKED EXAMPLES—A HISTORY PASSAGE

In 1941, an exuberant nationalist wrote: "We must accept wholeheartedly our duty and our opportunity as the most powerful and vital nation ... to exert upon the world the full impact of our influence, for such purposes as we see fit and by such means as we see fit." If forced to guess the identity of the writer, many US citizens would likely suspect a German jingoist advocating for *Lebensraum*. In actuality, the sentiment was expressed by one of America's own: Henry Luce, the highly influential publisher of the magazines *Life*, *Time*, and *Fortune*. Luce sought to dub the 1900s the "American Century," calling upon the nation to pursue global hegemony as it slipped from the grasp of warring Old World empires. As a forecast of world history, Luce's pronouncement seems prescient—but is it justifiable as a normative stance?

Not all of Luce's contemporaries bought into his exceptionalist creed. Only a year later, Henry Wallace, vice president under FDR, insisted that no country had the "right to exploit other nations" and that "military [and] economic imperialism" were invariably immoral. It is a foundational assumption in ethics that the wrongness of an act is independent of the particular identity of the actor—individuals who pay no heed to moral consistency are justly condemned as hypocrites. So why should it be any different for nation-states? In accord with this principle, Wallace proselytized for "the century of the common man," for the furtherance of a "great revolution of the people," and for bringing justice and prosperity to all persons irrespective of accidents of birth. Sadly, Wallace never had the chance to lead the United States in this cosmopolitan direction; prior to Roosevelt's demise at the beginning of his fourth term, the vice presidency was handed to Harry Truman, a man whose narrow provincialism ensconced him firmly in Luce's camp. And with Truman came the ghastly atomic eradication of two Japanese cities, the dangerous precedent set by military action without congressional approval in Korea, and a Cold War with the Soviet Union that brought the world to the brink of nuclear destruction.

MCAT Expertise

While the Denial Test will always reveal the correct answer in an Inference question, it's very time-consuming. If you cannot set good expectations for the right answer during the Execute step, triage the question and return to it later with the Denial Test.

Example:

1. One can most justifiably conclude on the basis of the author's discussion that Henry Luce assumed that:

   A. the United States did not have the right to create a military or economic empire.

   B. nation-states are never bounded by the same ethical principles that persons are.

   C. the same normative standards should apply to both Americans and Germans.

   D. moral rules that govern individual behavior do not necessarily apply to countries.

Solution: Assessing that this is an assumption is as easy as reading *assumed* at the end of the stem. You'll want to Plan to use the Denial Test, but first be clear on what Henry Luce's position is, particularly because he's not the only *Henry* discussed in the passage. Luce advocated for what the author calls the *exceptionalist* stance that the United States, as the most powerful country at the time, was free to do as it pleased. This is in contrast to Henry Wallace, who explicitly rebuffed Luce's view, so watch out for Faulty Uses of Detail that would actually describe Wallace.

Denying **choice (A)** yields *the United States* **did** *have the right to create a military or economic empire*, which is completely consistent with Luce's view. Eliminate it. As written, **choice (A)** is actually a view attributed to Wallace by the author, so it's both a FUD and an Opposite because it was the major point of disagreement between the two.

Choice (B) contains *never*, which is an extreme word, but because Luce seems to have a fairly strong position, you don't want to jump to labeling it a Distortion quite yet. It's a bit trickier to negate: to say that it is *not* the case that some event *never* happens is the same as saying the event *sometimes* occurs. Thus, the proper negation of **choice (B)** is *nation-states are* **sometimes** *bounded by the same ethical principles that persons are*, which is completely consistent with Luce, who presumably believes that ethical principles do apply to nations sometimes, say on those occasions when the nation in question is not the United States. Eliminate it.

For **choice (C)**, the contradiction would be *the same normative standards should **not** apply to both Americans and Germans*, which is again consistent with Luce's "American Century" idea. Hence, we can definitely cross off **choice (C)**, which, as written, is actually another one of Wallace's beliefs—a second Opposite/FUD combo.

All that remains is **choice (D)**, which does indeed destroy the argument if rejected. Countering it by saying *moral rules that operate on individuals **do** necessarily apply to countries* would mean that they *always* apply. But this supports the antihypocrisy argument that the author makes in favor of Wallace and against Luce at the beginning of paragraph 2. Thus, denying **choice (D)** would make Henry Luce's argument fall apart and so it is an assumption Luce has made. Discarded **choice (B)** was simply a more extreme version of this claim, rightly rejected as a Distortion because an author is more likely to assume a weak form of a statement than a strong one.

Bridge

Remember that the opposite of an Extreme Negative keyword (like *never*) is a Moderating Positive keyword (like *sometimes*). The circular view of Author keywords presented in Chapter 3 of *MCAT CARS Review* is a great way to visualize this change.

Example:

2. It is reasonable to infer that the author believes that:
    A. Harry Truman was the worst US president of the 20th century.
    B. Franklin Roosevelt did not endorse the idea of the "American Century."
    C. Henry Wallace would not have approved of the use of atomic weapons.
    D. Henry Luce did not provide an accurate historical assessment of the 1900s.

Solution: We can easily Assess this question as an Inference question given the phrase *reasonable to infer*. With a stem like this, which has no specific clues or references, you have little choice but to proceed with the Denial Test. It's not entirely clear what kind of inference this is because an author believes both assumptions and implications, but the same Plan can work for either, as noted above. While you can guess based on the author's descriptive language that she does not approve of Harry Truman, you do not know the writer's feelings toward any of the other American presidents in the 1900s, so denying that Truman was the absolute worst president would not have too much of an impact. **Choice (A)** is a Distortion, too extreme to attribute to the author.

For **choice (B)**, you do not really know what the author believes about Franklin Delano Roosevelt (FDR). We only know that he was the US president serving over both Wallace and Truman. Therefore we can make no safe inferences about FDR's attitude toward Luce's point of view: this Out of Scope option should be discarded.

Negate **choice (C)** and you arrive at *Henry Wallace **would** have approved of the use of atomic weapons*. If this were so, had he become president, he would have been guilty of the very misdeeds for which the author blames Truman—and the author would be utterly inconsistent in praising the one and condemning the other. In fact, because the author rails against hypocrisy, it is clear that she would have to hold the two men to the same ethical standards. Thus, denying **choice (C)** would considerably undermine the author's argument in paragraph two, and this is almost certainly the answer.

To make sure, finish Executing the Denial Test: rejecting **choice (D)** would have no negative impact—in fact, it would support the author's claim that Luce's view *seem[ed] prescient* as a historical prediction. This suggests that she indeed viewed Luce's view as historically accurate (even if ethically questionable). You can now be confident that **choice (C)** is the Answer.

10.2 Strengthen–Weaken (Within the Passage) Questions

MCAT Expertise

According to our research of released AAMC material, Strengthen–Weaken (Within the Passage) questions make up about 12 percent of questions in the CARS section (about six questions).

Strengthen–Weaken questions span two of AAMC's delineated categories, but both types generally concern the logical relationships between conclusions and the evidence that *strengthens* them or the refutations that *weaken* them. Recall that these relationships were discussed in depth in Chapters 5 and 6 of *MCAT CARS Review*, so return there if necessary. Note that the only substantial difference between Strengthen–Weaken (Within the Passage) and Strengthen–Weaken (Beyond the Passage) is that the former stick to the passage as written while the latter will bring in some new element, usually appearing in the question stem though on occasion only in the answer choices.

SAMPLE QUESTION STEMS

- The author's suggestion that [claim] is supported in the passage by:
- For which of the following statements from the passage does the author provide the most support?
- The author states in [paragraph reference] that [claim]. This most strengthens the author's contention that:

- Which of the following objections considered in the passage most WEAK-ENS the author's thesis?
- Which of the following is a claim that the author makes without providing evidence?
- The view of [person] is challenged in the passage by:
- How does other information from the passage relate to the claim that [quotation]?
- What significance does the assertion that [claim] have for the author's argument?

As this list suggests, these types of questions often contain references indicating that the answers will be taken directly from the text and are heavy on words indicating connections between claims like *relate*, *support*, and *challenge*. Some question stems may be ambiguous about whether the support or challenge you're looking for will be coming from in the text or outside of it, in which case you'll also want to bear in mind the strategy for Strengthen–Weaken (Beyond the Passage) questions detailed in the next chapter.

STRATEGY

Every Strengthen–Weaken question has three pieces: **two claims** and the **connection** between them. You will always be given at least one of these elements, and your task will be to find the other(s), so begin your Plan step by identifying where each piece can be found: either directly in the stem itself, somewhere in the passage, or in the answer choices.

If the *connection* is revealed in the question stem, it will typically be some variation of strengthen (support) or weaken (challenge), as the name of these questions suggest. However, when the connection does not occur until the answer choices, such as when a stem uses vague words like *relevance*, *significance*, or *impact*, the claims occasionally prove to have some other relationship such as identity (meaning the same thing) or even irrelevance. Once you know whether your task is to Strengthen, Weaken, or find some yet-to-be-discovered relevance, the next step of your Plan is to research the status of any *claims* quoted or otherwise referenced in the question stem. Your Execution could vary, based on the number of claims in the stem.

If no other claims are mentioned, such as in a question like *Which of the following passage assertions is the LEAST supported?*, you should probably just decide to triage after your initial Assessment of the question, resorting to process of elimination when you have time to Execute a Plan *later* in the section.

If two claims are referenced instead, then the task must be to find the nature of the relationship they share, so think about whether one claim stands under the other,

Key Concept

Evidence is used to support a conclusion through a one-way relationship. A refutation is used as a counterargument against a conclusion through a one-way relationship.

remembering that evidence makes a conclusion more likely to be true and refutations make conclusions less probable, as explained in Chapter 5 of *MCAT CARS Review*.

In most cases, though, you'll just be presented with one claim in the question stem, so Plan to identify the given statement as a conclusion, piece of evidence, or a refutation and then go to the passage, starting with the relevant sentence and looking in the surrounding text for language that suggests the appropriate relationship. Logic keywords are just about as important while you Execute the Plan as they are with Inference questions. If the question stem specified the relationship, pay special attention to that one; otherwise, just keep an eye out for any logical connections made to the claim, using those to set expectations.

If your initial Plan of attack proves unsuccessful, try process of elimination, crossing out any answer choice that does not establish the correct kind of relationship. Do not forget that support is unidirectional: if the "arrow" points the wrong way, it cannot be the right choice. So, for instance, if you are asked to find a claim that *supports* the author's thesis, a potential wrong answer is an implication that could be drawn if you assumed the thesis was true—in other words, a conclusion that the thesis itself *supported*.

WORKED EXAMPLES—AN ETHICS PASSAGE

The most prevalent argument against doctor-assisted suicide relies upon a distinction between *passive* and *active* euthanasia—in essence, the difference between killing someone and letting that person die. On this account, a physician is restricted by her Hippocratic oath to do no harm and thus cannot act in ways that would inflict the ultimate harm, death. In contrast, failing to resuscitate an individual who is dying is permitted because this would only be an instance of refraining from help and not a willful cause of harm. The common objection to this distinction, that it is vague and therefore difficult to apply, does not carry much weight. After all, applying ethical principles of *any sort* to the complexities of the world is an enterprise fraught with imprecision.

Rather, the fundamental problem with the distinction is that it is not an ethically relevant one, readily apparent in the following thought experiment. Imagine a terminally ill patient hooked up to an unusual sort of life support device, one that only functioned to prevent a separate "suicide machine" from administering a lethal injection so long as the doctor pressed a button on it once per day. Would there be any relevant difference between using the suicide machine directly and not using the prevention device? The intention of the doctor would be the same (fulfilling the patient's wish to die), and the effect would be the same (an injection causing the patient's death). The only variance here is the means by which the effect comes about, and this is not an ethical difference but merely a technical one.

Example:

3. Which of the following roles is played in the passage by the claim that the difference between killing and letting die is ethically relevant?

   I. It is contradicted by the assertion that the distinction between active and passive euthanasia is only technical.
   II. It bolsters the contention that applying ethical principles precisely is difficult.
   III. It underlies the most common argument against physician-assisted suicide.

   A. III only
   B. I and II only
   C. I and III only
   D. I, II, and III

Solution: The question asks about *roles* that are *played in the passage* by a statement given in the stem, so you can Assess that this is a Strengthen–Weaken (Within) question. However, it's a Roman numeral question, and these are usually more time-consuming. Your best bet is to save this for the end of the question set.

When you do work on it, Plan to start by locating the claim referenced in the question and leave the Roman numerals aside for now. As is often the case in more complex Strengthen–Weaken (Within) questions, there is no single sentence that contains all the words in the assertion; rather, parts of it are spread throughout the text. The two lines that are most important are the opening sentences of each paragraph, the first of which references *the difference between killing someone and letting that person die* and the second of which maintains that *the distinction ... is not an ethically relevant one.*

Just from this analysis, you can see first that the claim that the distinction is ethically relevant must be what is *relie[d] upon* (Evidence keyword) by the so-called *most prevalent argument against doctor-assisted suicide.* In other words, the claim that the distinction is ethically relevant plays a supporting role in that argument. Second, it is clear that the second paragraph is denying this claim. These initial observations already offer a sense of two roles that the distinction plays, a fairly thorough prediction.

MCAT Expertise

CARS authors often use multiple *terms* (words or phrases) to describe the same *concept*, or underlying idea. On Test Day, pay special attention to the ways in which authors use terms, especially when you see Opposition keywords, as discussed in Chapter 3 of *MCAT CARS Review*. When you come across dualisms, you can draw a set of columns adjacent to your map on your scratch paper and jot down what words the author uses for each side of the contrast. This can serve as a handy reference for any synonymous language you might encounter in the questions and answer choices. So, for the ethics passage, you would put *killing* and *active euthanasia* in one column and *letting die* and *passive euthanasia* in the other.

At this point, you can look at the answer choices to see how the Roman numerals are distributed. We generally recommend starting with the most common numeral or, alternatively, whichever seems easiest for you. Statements I and III both appear thrice, so start with the shorter of them. Statement III suggests the claim *underlies* the most common argument, which is precisely as predicted. Therefore, Statement III must be true and **choice (B)** can be crossed off.

Turning to Statement I, you'll note the mention of *the distinction between active and passive euthanasia*, which you were told in the first sentence was, *in essence, the difference between killing someone and letting that person die*. This is consistent with the expectation set earlier that the second paragraph challenges the assertion that the claim is ethically relevant. The final sentence confirms it: *this is not an ethical difference but merely a technical one*. The *not* tells you that this is the contradiction that Statement I suggests, so it must also be true, eliminating **choice (A)**.

There are still two answer choices remaining, so you will have to deal with Statement II. The contention that it mentions did not figure into our prediction, so check the text to find the reference, made at the end of the first paragraph. How does this assertion relate to the original claim that the distinction is ethically relevant? The clue is the keyword that precedes the assertion: *After all*. Even though it may sound like a Conclusion keyword on the surface, it's actually an Evidence keyword, which means that this assertion about *applying ethical principles* is in truth used to support something else. Specifically, this statement bolsters the author's belief that the *common objection* to the distinction carries little weight. This is not the relationship suggested by Statement II, which says that the claim that the distinction is ethically relevant supports how hard it is to apply ethical principles precisely. Thus, Statement II is false. Only Statements I and III are true, making **choice (C)** the correct answer.

Example:

4. On the basis of the author's discussion, which of the following items from the passage LEAST challenges the author's argument for the prohibition of active euthanasia?

  A. The thought experiment involving two suicide machines from the second paragraph

  B. The assertion that the distinction between passive and active euthanasia is too difficult to apply

  C. The argument that the distinction between passive and active euthanasia is only technical

  D. The claim that the effect and the intention are the same regardless of the type of euthanasia

Solution: Question 4 is somewhat tricky to untangle with quite a few negative terms, but you can quickly Assess that *challenges* and *from the passage* reveal this to be a Strengthen–Weaken (Within) question—specifically, Weaken. However, the *LEAST* means a **Scattered** format, one in which you'll probably have to test all of the answer choices. Save this for *later* if possible.

When Planning, begin by clarifying the *argument for the prohibition of active euthanasia*. Although the order after the dash in the first sentence is switched, it should be clear from the subsequent sentence that *active euthanasia* refers to the act of *killing*, which is supposedly forbidden because of the Hippocratic oath that the physician takes. This argument prohibiting active euthanasia is in fact that *most prevalent argument* from the first line. The correct answer, then, will be the one that challenges this argument the least.

The Scattered form suggests process of elimination, but before resorting to that, it doesn't hurt to see whether the author actually talks about a challenge that he regards poorly because that could be the very answer you're seeking. Indeed, the author does say in paragraph 1 that *the common objection ... does not carry much weight*. The objection referenced is that it's difficult to apply the distinction between killing and letting die, so this can serve as your prediction.

Looking at the answers, this matches with **choice (B)**. However, you should be cautious with this sort of question. While the passage says that the objection carries little weight, it does not say that it carries no weight at all, meaning that if there were an answer choice that had no effect or even supported the argument, that would be *even less* of a challenge. As it turns out, the remaining answer choices are all aspects of the counterargument made in the second paragraph, and all do indeed challenge the original argument. Now you can be confident that **choice (B)** is the correct answer.

10.3 Other *Reasoning Within the Text* Questions

There are a few rarer types of questions that do not neatly fall into either the Inference or Strengthen–Weaken (Within) categories, but that definitely concern passage reasoning and that do show up in some CARS sections. These can take many different forms and all are rare, so we'll just focus our discussion on three typical tasks.

CLARIFICATION

Questions that ask about **clarification** concern a relationship that is very similar to support, as it is also a one-way relationship. One assertion clarifies another if the two share roughly the same meaning, but the "clarifying" part is typically more specific or exact. Because the clarifying language tends to be more precise, its truth value is easier to assess, and thus you should think of "clarifying" statements as supporting evidence for "clarified" conclusions. Approach them more or less as you would a Strengthen–Weaken (Within) question, except keep in mind that the meanings should be roughly synonymous.

> **Key Concept**
>
> In a Clarification question, look for an answer choice that is nearly synonymous with the given claim, only that is more specific or exact.

With the ethics passage, for instance, you could see a Clarification question like *Which of the following clarifies the author's statement that the common argument against physician-assisted suicide rests upon the distinction between passive and active euthanasia?* The answer would most likely come from one of the sentences that followed, which explained the difference between the two more concretely, including the reasons why one is supposedly permitted and the other is not. In addition to words like *clarify*, words like *explain* and *reflect* are used in questions to indicate this kind of relationship.

WEAKNESS

Weakness questions are somewhat related to Inference questions, but they concern *implicit weaknesses* and *reasonable objections* to arguments discussed in the passage. Instead of the Denial Test, the best Plan is process of elimination by directly assessing the effect that answer choices have on the argument in question. The correct answer will have the most significant negative impact on the argument, perhaps even contradicting it altogether.

One example would be *Which of the following is the greatest inherent weakness in the author's use of a thought experiment to support the main argument?* This is a more complex type of *Reasoning Within the Text*, and it is one among a number of rarer questions that require you to appraise the strength of the author's reasoning.

The answer to this example might be the fact that thought experiments force the author to rely upon readers' imagination and intuition, which may not always result in the same conclusion as the author intended.

PARADOX

Finally, by a **paradox**, we mean an *apparent* logical contradiction, a set typically consisting of two assertions that seem inconsistent, but only at first glance. These will usually include two distinct claims from the text, phrased in a way to make them sound conflicting, followed by a question like *How would the author resolve this dilemma?* or *How might the passage account for this discrepancy?* Sometimes one of the claims will be a new element, which would technically make such questions *Reasoning Beyond the Text*, although they should still be approached with the same strategy in this case.

The correct answer to a Paradox question must be *consistent* with both of the claims given in the question stem. If possible, it should also not conflict with anything that the author says elsewhere in the passage. Thus, to resolve paradoxes, you should use process of elimination, marking out any answer choice that is inconsistent with one or both of the claims (or with the passage as a whole).

Conclusion

Although often variable in appearance, *Reasoning Within the Text* questions test only a few basic aptitudes: identifying necessary assumptions and inherent weaknesses in arguments; drawing probable inferences from stated claims; understanding relationships of consistency and conflict; and recognizing the connections in passages among conclusions, evidence, and refutations. Regardless of how challenging these questions may seem to you now, you have the ability to improve your reasoning skills! The solution is to practice using Logic keywords to identify support relationships, applying the Denial Test when appropriate, and applying the other strategies discussed in this chapter to your Plan of attack. These tactics will also be useful when working on the final class of questions, *Reasoning Beyond the Text*, the subject of the upcoming chapter.

CONCEPT AND STRATEGY SUMMARY

Inference Questions

- Assess: **Inference questions** look for unstated parts of arguments.

  ○ Unstated parts of arguments *must* be true given what is claimed in the passage.

  ○ **Assumptions** are unstated evidence.

  ○ **Implications** are unstated conclusions.

  ○ These questions often contain words like *assume*, *because*, *conclude*, *imply*, *infer*, *justify*, *reasonable*, or *suggest*.

- Plan: Determine whether you are looking for an assumption (evidence) or implication (conclusion). Then determine which claim the answer is supposed to support (assumptions) or be supported by (implications).

- Execute: Reread the relevant sentence, noting the explicit evidence and conclusions given.

  ○ For assumption questions, the answer is either similar to the evidence given or links the evidence to the conclusions.

  ○ For implication questions, the answer is either similar to the conclusions given or is another logical conclusion one could draw from the evidence.

- Answer: Match your expectations with the right answer. If there is no clear match, or if you cannot perform any of the earlier steps of the Kaplan Method for CARS Questions, use a special form of process of elimination called the Denial Test:

  ○ Negate each answer choice.

  ○ Whichever answer choice—when negated—has the most detrimental effect on the argument made in the passage is the correct answer choice.

Strengthen–Weaken (Within the Passage) Questions

- Assess: **Strengthen–Weaken (Within the Passage) questions** concern the logical relationship between conclusions and the evidence that strengthens them or the refutations that weaken them.

  ○ These questions often contain words like *relate*, *support*, *challenge*, *relevance*, *significance*, or *impact*.

  ○ These questions are closely related to Strengthen–Weaken (Beyond the Passage) questions, which simply bring in a new piece of information rather than using information directly from the passage.

- Plan: Determine the two claims and the connection between them; you will usually be given at least one of these elements and will have to find the other(s).

    o Identify where each piece of the argument can be found: in the question stem, in the passage, or in the answer choices.

    o If no claims are given in the question stem, Plan to triage it and answer it by process of elimination later.

    o If one claim is given in the question stem, determine if it is a conclusion, a piece of evidence, or a refutation.

    o If two claims are given in the question stem, identify the relationship between them.

- Execute: Research the relevant text to determine the missing claim or the connection between the claims. Use Logic keywords to help assemble the argument.

- Answer: Match your expectations with the right answer. If there is no clear match, or if you cannot perform any of the earlier steps of the Kaplan Method for CARS Questions, use process of elimination.

Other *Reasoning Within the Text* Questions

- **Clarification questions** ask for statements that are roughly synonymous, but the clarifying statement tends to be supporting evidence for the conclusion because it is more specific or exact.

    o These questions often contain words like *clarify*, *explain*, or *reflect*.

    o Approach these questions as you would Strengthen–Weaken (Within) questions, except that the meanings of the two claims should be roughly synonymous.

- **Weakness questions** ask for implicit refutations to arguments discussed in the passage.

    o These questions often contain words like *implicit weaknesses* or *reasonable objections*.

    o Approach these questions using the Denial Test for Inference questions, except that the correct answer will be the most detrimental to the argument made in the passage *without* being negated.

- **Paradox questions** ask for the resolution of an apparent logical contradiction.

    o These questions often contain words like *paradox*, *dilemma*, or *discrepancy*.

    o Approach these questions through the process of elimination, crossing out any answer choice that is inconsistent with one or both of the claims of the paradox or with the passage as a whole.

11

Question Types III:
Reasoning Beyond the Text Questions

In This Chapter

Introduction

If patients came with instruction manuals, medical school might not be necessary. Many of the clinical tasks you will perform as a physician require applying the vast quantities of knowledge you will master over your years of medical school to situations that never quite match the ones you read about in class. When real-life patients are conscious and able to describe their symptoms, the language they use rarely coincides with the sophisticated terminology employed in textbooks and journals. Consequently, much of medical training involves actual patient interactions, transcending the classroom to include lessons that can only be taught at the bedside. Medical schools are interested in students who know how to go beyond what they've read, which is why the *Critical Analysis and Reasoning Skills* (CARS) section makes this a major focus. Although it may not be the intensive care unit, the MCAT is like the ICU in that both test whether you understand what you think you've learned well enough to apply it with both speed and precision.

In this chapter, we'll examine the Apply and Strengthen–Weaken (Beyond the Passage) question types. As in the previous question types chapters, we'll look at some common question stems, specific strategies, and a few worked examples for each question type. We conclude with a brief discussion of rarer kinds of *Reasoning Beyond the Text* questions.

The AAMC reports that 40 percent of the questions in the CARS section should be classified as *Reasoning Beyond the Text*, and it further divides this categorization into questions that require you to apply or extrapolate ideas from the passage to a new context (Apply questions) and those that require you to evaluate the effect new

Bridge

Apply and Strengthen–Weaken (Beyond the Text) are examples of deductive reasoning at its finest. In both cases, a new situation is provided. In Apply questions, we focus on how the passage relates to the new information (through a Response, Outcome, or Example). In Strengthen–Weaken (Beyond) questions, we focus on how the new information impacts the passage. Deductive reasoning, and other problem-solving techniques, are discussed in Chapter 4 of *MCAT Behavioral Sciences Review*.

information would have if incorporated into the passage. (Because the effect typically takes one of two forms, we call these Strengthen–Weaken (Beyond the Passage) questions.) In other words, the fundamental difference is one of direction: Apply questions go from passage to new situation, while Strengthen–Weaken (Beyond) questions go from new situation to passage. While the AAMC seems to suggest that the *Reasoning Beyond the Text* category is split evenly between these, according to our intensive study of released AAMC materials, Apply questions appear to be a bit more common than Strengthen–Weaken (Beyond) questions. So, out of the approximately 21 *Reasoning Beyond* questions you'll see in a CARS section, typically about 11 will be Apply questions, and only about 8 or 9 will be Strengthen–Weaken (Beyond) questions, with perhaps 1 that doesn't neatly fall into either type.

Note: The Question Types, as well as the Kaplan Method for CARS Passages, Kaplan Method for CARS Questions, and Wrong Answer Pathologies are included as tear-out sheets in the back of this book.

11.1 Apply Questions

Questions that fall into the broad category of *Reasoning Beyond the Text* are easy to identify because they always involve novel information (in the question stem, set of answer choices, or both) that is not stated or even suggested by the passage and that may not even seem to be related at first. In one typical pattern, words like *Suppose*, *Assume*, and *Imagine* precede an elaborate scenario that fills several lines of text, followed up with a question that connects this new content to the author or passage. There are two basic ways in which this connection may be asked about, varying with respect to the direction in the relationship: passage → new situation or new situation → passage. The first make up the Apply question type, while the second constitute Strengthen–Weaken (Beyond) questions.

Apply questions are the most common of the eight major types discussed in these three chapters. They take the text as a starting point and ask you to extrapolate to a new context. While the questions posed can vary considerably, there are three frequently occurring tasks, each of which constitutes roughly one-third of the Apply question pool: we call them *Response*, *Outcome*, and *Example*, reflecting some of the words they commonly contain.

MCAT Expertise

According to our research of released AAMC material, Apply questions make up about 21 percent of the CARS section (about 11 questions).

SAMPLE QUESTION STEMS

- Consider the following: [new info]. The author would most likely respond to this by claiming:
- With which of the following claims would [the author or an alternative viewpoint from the passage] be LEAST likely to agree?

- Suppose that [details of new scenario]. Based on the passage, what would the author most probably advise in such a scenario?
- Imagine [new info]. Which of the following, according to information presented in the passage, is the most reasonable outcome?
- If the passage's author is correct, the most likely consequence of [new situation] would be:
- Assume that [new info]. One could reasonably expect, on the basis of the passage, that:
- Which of the following best exemplifies the author's notion of [quotation from the passage]?
- Which of the following phenomena would the author most likely characterize as a [concept]?
- [New info]. The author would most likely classify this as:

At least a third of Apply questions look like the first three, concerning how the author (or, less frequently, some other individual or a proponent of a theory discussed in the passage) would respond to a particular situation. Besides asking for the likely *response* or *reply*, these questions may simply ask for a claim that the author would be *most likely to agree with* or the statement *least consistent with* one of the views discussed.

Other Apply questions are like the next three, investigating the most probable *outcome*, *result*, *expectation*, or *consequence* in a situation that is in some way analogous to that discussed in the passage. In other words, these questions give you a cause and ask about what effect is likely if the passage is believed.

Finally, most of the remaining third of Apply questions are like the final three cases, asking for *examples* or *instances* of ideas discussed in the passage. More often, the concept will be given and you'll have to find an item from a specified context (or from the "real world") that would provide the best example of that term as the author uses it. Rarer and more difficult are questions like the last one, which start with the outside case and ask you how the author would categorize it: *What is this an example of?*

STRATEGY

If new information is provided in the question stem, you may find it advantageous to jump to the colon or question mark at the end to see what the question is really asking. Once you've picked up on the key language to Assess your task, read any new information in the question stem closely for hints that connect it to the passage. Then go back and reread the relevant portions to make your prediction. When Planning, keep in mind the type of Apply involved.

MCAT Expertise

Whenever a question stem is particularly lengthy, it is almost certainly going to involve *Reasoning Beyond the Text*, but it could just as easily be Apply as Strengthen–Weaken (Beyond). To save time on Test Day, whenever you see many lines of new information, perhaps preceded by clues like *Suppose*, *Imagine*, or *Assume*, take a moment to jump ahead to the very last line before the question mark or colon at the end to determine which of the two types of question this is and precisely what is it that you'll be looking for. After you have a better idea of your task, Plan to read through the new information carefully, always watching out for analogies to and similarities with the passage text.

Response

If the stem asks for how the author would Respond or a claim the author would be likely to endorse, your task will be to get inside the author's head. The correct answer to a Response question should be consistent with the author's beliefs, which are typically reflected in the passage through the use of Author keywords, originally discussed in Chapter 3 of *MCAT CARS Review*. If you find yourself with an unhelpful prediction, eliminate any answers that would be logically inconsistent with the author's assertions. If a viewpoint other than the author's is asked about, follow a similar strategy by putting yourself in the mindset of the alternative perspective mentioned in the stem.

Outcome

With questions that ask about the probable Outcomes of scenarios, you'll want to pay more attention to language in the passage that deals with cause and effect, much of which will be Logic keywords. Identify any causes in the passage that are analogous to what is presented in the question stem and use the effects for which they are said to be responsible as the basis for your prediction.

Example

In those cases when you are called upon to identify Examples, find the relevant text from the passage, especially any text that provides definitions, explanations, or the author's own examples of the concept in question. Take note of necessary conditions (which must occur in all instances of the concept) and sufficient conditions (which are enough on their own to make an instance qualify as that concept), both originally discussed in Chapter 6 of *MCAT CARS Review*. Sufficient conditions allow for quicker matches, but necessary conditions can be used to rule out answers that lack them in a process of elimination.

WORKED EXAMPLES—A PSYCHOLOGY PASSAGE

There is no shortage of evidence for the existence of systemic biases in ordinary human reasoning. For instance, Kahneman and Tversky in their groundbreaking 1974 work proposed the existence of a heuristic—an error-prone shortcut in reasoning—known as "anchoring." In one of their most notable experiments, participants were exposed to the spin of a roulette wheel (specially rigged to land randomly on one of only two possible results) before being asked to guess what percent of United Nations member states were African. The half of the sample who had the roulette wheel stop at 65 guessed, on average, that 45% of the UN was African, while those with a result of 10 guessed only 25%, demonstrating that prior presentation of a random number otherwise unconnected to a quantitative judgment can still influence that judgment.

Bridge

Does the content of this passage look familiar? Heuristics are simplified principles used to make decisions; they are colloquially called "rules of thumb." Bias is a systematic error made in reasoning. These topics are discussed in Chapter 4 of *MCAT Behavioral Sciences Review*.

The anchoring effect has been observed on repeated other occasions, such as in Dan Ariely's experiment that used digits in Social Security numbers as an anchor for bids at an auction, and in the 1996 study by Wilson et al. that showed even awareness of the existence of anchoring bias is insufficient to mitigate its effects. The advertising industry has long been aware of this bias, the rationale for its frequent practice of featuring an "original" price before showing a "sale" price that is invariably reduced. Of course, anchoring is hardly alone among the defective tendencies in human reasoning; other systemic biases have also been experimentally identified, including loss aversion, the availability heuristic, and optimism bias.

Example:

1. Suppose a consumer who is looking for an inexpensive replacement for her outmoded refrigerator is drawn by a local retailer's ads for a discount sale promising savings of 50 percent or greater on all appliances. The author would probably warn the consumer that:

   A. sales are scams designed to exploit the consuming public.

   B. the pre-markdown prices are most likely set artificially high.

   C. heavily discounted merchandise is likely damaged or stolen.

   D. making a rational decision about what to buy is impossible.

Solution: With the lengthy question stem, it's worth your while to jump to the part immediately before the colon to Assess what kind of *Reasoning Beyond the Text* will be required. In this case, you're tasked with determining what the author would warn, a kind of Response, which means we want to be thinking about views that the author holds. The ads for the sale should draw you to paragraph two, in which the author states, *The advertising industry has long been aware of this bias, the rationale for its frequent practice of featuring an "original" price before showing a "sale" price that is invariably reduced*. Although the author is not explicit, the use of quotation marks here is a case of "scare quotes," suggesting that the so-called "original" price is just there to make the "sale" price seem lower. Thus, it's reasonable to infer that the author would warn the consumer about the anchoring effect intended with presale prices.

The closest match to this prediction is **choice (B)**, which actually comes quite close. **Choice (A)** can be ruled out as a Distortion because the language is just too strong. Any advice or admonitions that an author would provide should be consistent with what the author says in the passage, but they should also share a similar tone. The author here is not so condemning of this advertising practice as to endorse a suggestion like **choice (A)**. Answer **choice (D)** is also a Distortion because of the word *impossible*. Finally, **choice (C)** is Out of Scope. The author suggests that discounts are offered to manipulate buyers into believing they have found a better deal, not to trick them into buying products that turn out to be faulty.

Example:

2. Imagine that a psychologist specialized in the study of systemic reasoning biases. On the basis of the information presented, this psychologist could most reasonably be expected to:

   A. have a higher likelihood of misjudging numerical quantities when not given an anchor.

   B. make significantly fewer mistakes in reasoning than those ignorant of anchoring bias.

   C. be equally as susceptible to errors resulting from the anchoring effect as anyone else.

   D. avoid entirely the logical fallacies that ordinary human beings commit systematically.

Solution: The question stem is relatively short, so there's no need to jump to the end before reading the part after *Imagine*. Because we're searching for something *this psychologist could most reasonably be expected to* do, you can Assess the task as finding an Outcome. Does the passage suggest anything about what happens to psychologists with greater knowledge of these biases in reasoning? There is no explicit reference, and the question stem is not heavy on other clues to facilitate much of a prediction. With a question like this, Plan to start examining the answer choices to look for additional clues about how the passage can help you.

The very first possibility suggests a consequence that would occur without the presentation of an anchor. However, the passage only concerns what happens when an anchor is present; it tells us nothing about how accurate people's judgments of quantities are without the anchoring effect. We therefore have zero basis for deciding what effect having no anchor has. Eliminate **choice (A)** as Out of Scope.

Choice **(B)** suggests that such a psychologist would make many fewer mistakes because of her knowledge of the anchoring effect. Is there anything in the passage that would warrant such a conclusion? In fact, you discover quite the contrary. In the second paragraph, the author states that Wilson and his colleagues *showed even awareness of the existence of anchoring bias is insufficient to mitigate its effects*. Not only does this rule out **choice (B)** as an Opposite, but it also gives you an idea of what would make for a correct answer—one that says this psychologist is just as likely as anybody else to fall into these errors due to anchoring.

This revision to your Plan pays off when you read **choice (C)**, which is almost an exact match for the new prediction. On Test Day, you would select this choice and move on to the next question without paying much attention to **choice (D)**—which could be ruled out for being a Distortion or an Opposite, constituting an even more extreme version of **choice (B)**.

MCAT Expertise

Although we generally recommend as a first Plan of attack that you make a prediction before looking at any of the answer options, with *Reasoning Beyond the Text* questions that contain new elements in the answers, sometimes looking at the first one or two can give you a better idea of the form that the correct answer will take. If you find that the options diverge significantly from what you expected, it's advisable to go back and modify your original expectations before moving on to any remaining choices. As explained in Chapter 8 of *MCAT CARS Review*, matching to the correct answer is generally less time-consuming than crossing out all three incorrect ones, so revising your prediction is usually a more optimal strategy than process of elimination.

Example:

3. Which of the following would the author be LEAST likely to consider a case of anchoring bias?
   A. An unusually high opening bid at an annual charity auction leads to a sizable increase over previous years in total proceeds collected.
   B. The sequel to a popular film is deemed a failure because it could not quite beat the record-smashing box office receipts of the original.
   C. A shipping website receives reports of greater levels of customer satisfaction after starting deliberately to overestimate delivery times.
   D. Poor initial sales figures for a new video game console motivate its manufacturer to reduce significantly the system's suggested retail price.

Solution: Despite asking for the *LEAST likely* case, this is still an Example question. While it's hard to know what to predict based on the limited information in the question stem, you can still set expectations about the correct answer by Planning to investigate the concept mentioned. The anchoring effect is the primary subject of this short passage, but the author only provides examples of the phenomenon without giving it an explicit definition. It's difficult to say precisely what would be sufficient to constitute anchoring bias, but we can isolate some necessary conditions. In each of the passage examples, a baseline numerical expectation or "anchor" is set (either at random, as in the case of the experiments mentioned, or deliberately high in order to manipulate purchasers), which then skews the judgments people make about quantities. Any answer choice that satisfies these prerequisites should be eliminated because you are asked to find the *LEAST likely* example.

Choice (A) is clearly a case of the anchoring effect; the passage even made mention of an experiment that used bids at an auction as the dependent variable. You can reason that the lofty opening bid must have caused other participants to heighten their appraisals of the items for sale, which in turn led to larger final sale prices and increased total proceeds.

Even though **choice (B)** is unlike anything found directly in the passage, it nevertheless seems to follow the model we anticipated for wrong answers. In this case, the original film is serving as the anchor that biases judgments of its sequel. That the new movie *could not quite beat the record-smashing box office receipts of the original* suggests that it still generated a lot of revenue, meaning that the assessment of failure was probably in error. Because the anchoring effect is said to be a systematic bias, this implication of error should quell any remaining doubts about eliminating **choice (B)**.

Turning to **choice (C)**, we find another case that departs considerably from the passage. Here, the anchor would be the estimated time of arrival for a particular shipment. If the site deliberately overestimates shipping times, that means its customers will consistently have to wait less time than they are told to expect, which will lead many to think that they are receiving excellent service. This is precisely analogous to the example of the original price marked down for sale, and hence it should also be eliminated.

This entails that the correct answer is **choice (D)**. While similar to one of the examples discussed on a superficial level, it does not fit the model of anchoring bias that we articulated. The monetary value of the sales (which would undoubtedly be orders of magnitude higher than the original price of one individual console) does not *bias* the manufacturer to lower the cost per system. Rather, this is a case of a rational response to an economic problem: when demand is too low, reduce the price.

Now, to be clear, this reduction in price could *lead to* a case of anchoring bias if, say, consumers started to purchase the console in greater quantities, believing it now to be a better deal. But the answer choice does not focus on that effect or on any of the effects of cutting the cost, rather only mentioning its cause. And so, **choice (D)** is indubitably the one least likely to count as anchoring bias for the author.

11.2 Strengthen–Weaken (Beyond the Passage) Questions

Like the similarly named category detailed in the preceding chapter, **Strengthen–Weaken (Beyond the Passage) questions** concern evidence–conclusion relationships. However, unlike the other type of Strengthen–Weaken question, at least one of the claims involved will not be from the passage but will be unique to the question stem or answer choices. Strengthen–Weaken (Beyond) questions are also distinct because they treat the passage as flexible, subject to modification by outside forces.

SAMPLE QUESTION STEMS

- Suppose [new info]. This new information:
- Which of the following statements, if true, would most bolster the author's argument about [topic]?
- Assume that [new info]. This assumption weakens the author's claim that:
- [New info] would most strongly support the view of:
- Recent research on [topic] suggests [new info]. Which of the following assertions from the passage is most logically consistent with these results?
- Some theorists have argued that [new info]. Based on the discussion in the passage, which of the following would present the greatest CHALLENGE to their argument?
- [New info]. In conjunction with information presented in the passage, it would be most reasonable to conclude that:
- Imagine that [new info]. What impact would this have on the arguments made in the passage?
- Which of the following study findings would most seriously undermine the author's thesis?

If the question includes new information and asks about logical relationships like support, challenge, and consistency, you can safely Assess that it's a Strengthen–Weaken (Beyond) question. However, sometimes the new information is hidden in the answer choices, so you may have to watch out for clues that suggest the correct answer will come from outside the passage, such as words like *would* and *could*.

STRATEGY

As with Strengthen–Weaken (Within the Passage) questions, your primary task will be to identify the three relevant parts: the conclusion, the evidence or refutation, and the nature of the connection (strengthen, weaken, or some unspecified relevance). Your first step should be to determine which component (or, rarely, which two components) you'll be seeking. If the stem is long, don't bother to read all the

MCAT Expertise

According to our research of released AAMC material, Strengthen–Weaken (Beyond the Passage) questions make up about 16 percent of the CARS section (about eight or nine questions).

Bridge

Strengthen–Weaken (Beyond the Passage) questions are extremely similar to Strengthen–Weaken (Within the Passage) questions, except that the former bring in new information while the latter ask about arguments wholly contained in the passage. Accordingly, the strategic approaches to these two types of questions are very similar. Make sure to review Strengthen–Weaken (Within) questions, discussed in Chapter 10 of *MCAT CARS Review*, in tandem with this discussion of Strengthen–Weaken (Beyond) questions.

new details the first time through. Instead, jump to what immediately precedes the question mark or colon in order to figure out where the question stem is going. With this Plan in mind, turn next to what you are given, reading the entire question stem closely now and keeping an eye out for any hints of analogy. So, for instance, if a novel experimental finding described in the question stem reminds you of a study in the passage that was used to support the author's thesis, then chances are that the correct answer will indicate that this *strengthens* the thesis, or a similar idea.

From this point, the same strategy considerations apply as did to Strengthen–Weaken (Within) questions, with Logic keywords from the passage again playing a major role. The major differences will be that correct answers to Strengthen–Weaken (Beyond) questions are seldom exact matches to your predictions and are far more likely to be only incidentally related to the text.

WORKED EXAMPLES—AN ARTS PASSAGE

One of the first examples of the ascendance of abstraction in 20th-century art is the Dada movement, which Lowenthal dubbed "the groundwork to abstract art and sound poetry, a starting point for performance art, a prelude to postmodernism, an influence on pop art…and the movement that laid the foundation for surrealism." Dadaism was ultimately premised on a philosophical rejection of the dominant culture, which is to say the dominating culture of colonialist Europe. Not content with the violent exploitation of other peoples, the gaze of Europe's ruling factions once again turned inward, reigniting provincial disputes into the conflagration that came to be known by the Eurocentric epithet "World War I"—the European subcontinent apparently being the only part of the world that mattered.

The absurd destructiveness of the Great War was a natural prelude to the creative absurdity of Dada. Is it any wonder that the rejection of reason made manifest by senseless atrocities should lead to the embrace of irrationality and disorder among the West's subaltern artistic communities? Marcel Janco, one of the first Dadaists, cited this rationale: "We had lost confidence in our culture. Everything had to be demolished. We would begin again after the *tabula rasa*." Thus, we find the overturning of what was once considered art: a urinal becomes the *Fountain* after Marcel Duchamp signs it "R. Mutt" in 1917, the nonsense syllables of Hugo Ball and Kurt Schwitters transform into "sound poems," dancers in cardboard cubist costumes accompanied by foghorns and typewriters metamorphosize into the ballet *Parade*. Unsurprisingly, many commentators, including founding members, have described Dada as an "anti-art" movement. Notwithstanding such a designation, Dadaism has left a lasting imprint on modern Western art.

Example:

4. According to some estimates, prior to the beginning of World War I in 1914, more than four-fifths of the world's landmass was controlled by European nations or former colonies such as the United States. If this figure is accurate, what effect does it have on the passage?

   A. It bolsters the author's suggestion that European colonialism was an overbearing force.

   B. It weakens the author's assertion that World War I was instigated by provincial disputes.

   C. It strengthens the author's claim that Europe is the only place in the world that mattered.

   D. It challenges the author's insinuation that European rulers ignored the rest of the globe.

Solution: With lengthy opening details, you'll want to skip right to the question itself, which asks for the *effect* on the passage. Assess that this is a Strengthen–Weaken (Beyond) question and that your task will be to determine the relevance of this new data. As you read the stem a second time, now closely, think about how the information presented either supports or challenges statements from the passage. The evidence provided has nothing to do directly with the Dada movement, which doesn't even start until after the commencement of the war, but it does pertain to the author's discussion of Europe and World War I at the end of the first paragraph, so Executing your Plan requires rereading that portion of the text to see whether anything there would be impacted. If nothing else, the figure cited does seem to support the author's opinionated characterization of *the dominating culture of colonialist Europe*.

If you look for a match, you'll find that **choice (A)** works perfectly. The word *overbearing* is just a synonym for *dominating*, so there is a close connection with language actually used in the passage. On Test Day, you would select this answer and then move on to the next question without even bothering to read the wrong answers.

For our purposes, however, it's worth reviewing where the others go wrong. **Choice (B)** may point to a claim that the author actually makes, but the fact from the question stem does not really pose a threat to it. Regardless of how much landmass each country controlled, the catalyst for World War I could remain disputes among these countries. This answer is a Faulty Use of Detail. In contrast, **choice (C)** is wrong for two reasons: first, it's Out of Scope because this is not something the author endorses; the phrase *the European subcontinent apparently being the only part of the world that mattered* is used almost sarcastically when the author points out that "World" War I actually took place exclusively in Europe. Second, even if the author did have this view, the statement is a value judgment—a matter of opinion—which cannot be directly affected by geographic facts. Finally, **choice (D)** does contain a factual claim that would be challenged by the question stem. The only problem is that this is not an insinuation of the author's, who explicitly references the rulers *turn[ing] inward* after *violent exploitation of other peoples*, suggesting they were indeed gazing outward before the start of the war, the time period noted in the question stem. It's also Out of Scope.

Example:

5. Which of the following, if true, would most threaten what the author says in the final sentence of the second paragraph?
    A. A large majority of members of the general public, when asked to identify the most important work of art of the 1900s, fail to mention an example from the Dada movement.
    B. Other prominent 20th-century artistic movements, such as Surrealism and Pop Art, were also commonly described as "anti-art" by their most influential participants.
    C. The consensus among art historians today is that Dada was merely a brief departure from the principal themes in European art that evolved during the 20th-century.
    D. Some of the founding members of the Dada movement were sympathetic to the radical view that, far from being anti-art, Dada was the purest form of art imaginable.

Solution: Although this question is perhaps more difficult to Assess than the previous example, the hypothetical *if true* is strong evidence that the answer choices will be new elements and that this is indeed a Strengthen–Weaken (Beyond) question. Clearly the task is to Weaken the author's claim; *threaten* is just a less common way of saying this.

Plan to follow the reference in the stem and reread that last line, as well as the preceding one to gain additional context. The penultimate sentence (the one before the last) suggests that some people think of Dada as *anti-art*, but the last one contests this by noting Dada's *lasting imprint on modern Western art*. Thus, we are most likely looking for a refutation of the author's idea that Dada was influential.

There is a chance, however, that the correct answer challenges the author's rejection of the term *anti-art*. In other words, if we cancel out the confusing double negatives, the correct answer could be one that supports the idea that Dada is anti-art.

An elaborate prediction, such as the one just formulated, will usually result in a quicker match. In this case, we find it in **choice (C)**. An appeal to expert opinion is often an acceptable form of evidence for arts and literary passages, as can be seen here in the author's name-dropping and quotation-citing, so consensus among experts should carry even more weight. The scholars' idea of a *brief departure* clashes directly with the *lasting imprint* from the text, so we can be confident in identifying **choice (C)** as correct.

You would ordinarily want to move on to the next question at this point, but it's worth learning about the flaws in the wrong options. **Choice (A)** clearly does not support what the author says, but it poses less of a challenge than it may seem to. For one, popular opinion could easily be mistaken about how influential particular works of art are. But, more substantially, leaving a *lasting imprint* is not identical to being the singularly most important movement of the century. Thus, the threat presented by **choice (A)** is extremely weak at best. The remaining options are Opposites that actually support the author. **Choice (B)** is completely consistent with the passage, strengthening the point that simply calling a movement *anti-art* does not necessarily make it so. **Choice (D)** has no impact on the passage. Even if some of the founding members of Dadaism did not think of the movement as being anti-art, many of the founding members certainly could have held this view. Further, this answer choice attempts to weaken the penultimate sentence—not the last one of the paragraph.

MCAT Expertise

Appeals to authority or expert opinion are common in CARS passages, particularly those involving disciplines like the arts or literature, in which value judgments and other opinions play a prominent role. Widespread agreement among experts, though rare in these fields, would of course provide even stronger support. That said, be mindful of the field that you are reading about and the types of argumentation that the author chooses to employ. Quoting experts may provide decent support for a passage on an artistic movement, but such testimony will carry far less weight in more empirical social sciences like psychology or economics. Non-expert opinions tend to carry even less weight: while authors may occasionally draw on popular opinion to support arguments, actual surveys of public opinion are seldom seen outside of a small number of cases, confined primarily to political science.

11.3 Other *Reasoning Beyond the Text* Questions

A handful of question tasks that transcend the passage fall into neither the Strengthen–Weaken (Beyond) nor Apply types. Because none of these occurs especially frequently, we will simply discuss three cases that have made an appearance on past MCAT exams.

PROBABLE HYPOTHESIS

In many ways, **Probable Hypothesis questions** are a counterpart to Apply questions that ask about Outcomes, inquiring instead about the likely causes of the

MCAT Expertise

According to our research of released AAMC material, there is usually one *Reasoning Beyond the Text* question that is neither an Apply nor a Strengthen–Weaken (Beyond the Passage) question.

new situations discussed. After presenting the new details, these stems will ask for *a probable hypothesis*, *the likely cause*, or *the most reasonable explanation based on the passage*. Working backward from a given effect to its probable cause can be more difficult, but again your task will be to use the Logic keywords that reveal analogous cause–effect relationships in the passage to form your prediction. If no match can be found, eliminate any answers that contradict claims the author states or suggests elsewhere in the passage.

ALTERNATIVE EXPLANATION

Alternative Explanation questions also concern causes. However, what makes these questions tricky is that they start with a phenomenon that might be directly from the passage but ask for a cause that is not given and that may not even be that similar to anything discussed. Such questions are almost impossible to predict, so Plan to go through each answer choice, eliminating any that would not produce the result given in the stem. If stuck between multiple answers that seem just about equally likely to serve as the cause, eliminate those that would most conflict with other parts of the passage. A correct alternative explanation won't be one that the author provides, but, other than departing from the author's original explanation, it should not significantly contradict the author.

PASSAGE ALTERATION

One other less common *Reasoning Beyond the Text* question type will inquire about changes that the author could make to the passage to allow it to be consistent with new information provided. These are appropriately called **Passage Alteration questions**. In many ways, these are like the rare instances of *Reasoning Within the Text* that require resolving paradoxes, except that they will include some new information that contradicts what the author says or implies. The correct answer to these questions will typically be the one that produces the desired effect with the *least* amount of modification to ideas originally presented in the passage.

Conclusion

And so this brings us to the end of our discussion of question types. If you still find yourself confused about which name corresponds to which type, don't worry! The common stems, tailored strategies, and worked examples of the last three chapters are only designed to be your first exposure to the intricacies of the Kaplan Method for CARS questions, the question types and tasks, and the Wrong Answer Pathologies. Continue practicing until the Method becomes second nature for you. In the end, it will be less important to be able to simply name the question type, and it will be more important to know what to do with such a question. The number one best way to improve your performance with CARS questions and get that higher score you deserve is practice accompanied by effective review—the subject of our final chapter.

CONCEPT AND STRATEGY SUMMARY

Apply Questions

- Assess: **Apply questions** require you to take the information given in the passage and extrapolate it to a new context. Apply questions may ask for one of three tasks.

  ○ They may ask for the author's **Response** to a situation, using words like *response, reply, most likely to agree with,* or *least consistent with*.

  ○ They may ask for the most probable **Outcome** in a situation, using words like *outcome, result, expectation,* or *consequence*.

  ○ They may ask for an **Example** of an idea discussed in the passage, using words like *example* or *instance*.

  ○ These questions often begin with words like *Suppose, Consider,* or *Imagine*.

- Plan: If the question stem is long, jump to the end to determine what it's asking. Read any information given in the question stem closely, looking for hints that connect it to the passage.

- Execute: Reread the relevant text, keeping in mind the specific type of Apply question involved.

  ○ For Response questions, determine the author's key beliefs, which are generally reflected in the passage using Author keywords.

  ○ For Outcome questions, pay attention to cause–effect relationships in the passage, which are generally reflected in the passage using Logic keywords.

  ○ For Example questions, look for text that provides definitions, explanations, or the author's own example, noting any necessary or sufficient conditions.

- Answer: Match your expectations with the right answer. If there is no clear match, or if you cannot perform any of the earlier steps of the Kaplan Method for CARS Questions, use process of elimination.

  ○ Eliminate any answer choices that are inconsistent with the author's views, especially for Response questions.

  ○ Eliminate any answer choice that does not contain necessary conditions (which must occur in all instances of a concept), especially for Example questions.

Strengthen–Weaken (Beyond the Passage) Questions

- Assess: **Strengthen–Weaken (Beyond the Passage) questions** concern the logical relationship between conclusions and the evidence that strengthens them or the refutations that weaken them.

  - These questions often contain words like *relate*, *support*, *challenge*, *relevance*, *significance*, or *impact*. In contrast to Strengthen–Weaken (Within the Passage) questions, they often contain words like *could* or *would*.

  - These questions are closely related to Strengthen–Weaken (Within the Passage) questions, which use information directly from the passage, rather than bringing in a new piece of information.

  - Read the question stem closely, looking for hints of analogy to parts of the passage.

- Plan: Determine the two claims and the connection between them; you will usually be given at least one of these elements and will have to find the other(s).

  - Identify where each piece of the argument can be found: in the question stem, in the passage, or in the answer choices.

  - If no claims are given in the question stem, plan to triage it and answer it by process of elimination later.

  - If one claim is given in the question stem, determine if it is a conclusion, a piece of evidence, or a refutation.

  - If two claims are given in the question stem, identify the relationship between them.

- Execute: Research the relevant text to determine the missing claim or the connection between them. Use Logic keywords to help assemble the argument.

- Answer: Match your expectations with the right answer. If there is no clear match, or if you cannot perform any of the earlier steps of the Kaplan Method for CARS Questions, use process of elimination.

Other *Reasoning Beyond the Text* Questions

- **Probable Hypothesis questions** ask for causes of new situations presented in the question stem.

  - These questions often contain words like *probable hypothesis*, *likely cause*, or *most reasonable explanation*.

  - Approach these questions like Apply questions, except that you are looking for analogous cause–effect relationships in the passage.

- **Alternative Explanation questions** ask for causes that differ from the ones given in the passage but that still provide an explanation for a phenomenon.
  - These questions often contain words like *alternative explanation*, *other cause*, or *different reason*.
  - Approach these questions by eliminating any answer choice that would not lead to the effect in the question stem. If stuck between multiple answers, eliminate those that conflict most significantly with the passage.
- **Passage Alteration questions** ask for changes the author could make to the passage to make it consistent with new information.
  - These questions often contain words like *alter*, *change*, or *update*.
  - Approach these questions by looking for the answer that produces the desired effect with the least amount of modification to the ideas in the passage.

Effective Review of CARS

In This Chapter

Introduction

This final chapter is a troubleshooting guide for raising your score. Practice the strategies discussed throughout this book, especially the Kaplan Method for CARS Passages from Chapter 4 of *MCAT CARS Review* and the Kaplan Method for CARS Questions from Chapter 8. Start by working on some practice passages and questions from Full-Length Exams or other materials in your online Kaplan resources. Using these online resources is a prerequisite for any of the review strategies discussed in this chapter to be effective. We'll look at five proven ways to increase your *Critical Analysis and Reasoning Skills* (CARS) section score—including some methods you'll find useful for the science sections as well!

Hands down, the best way to improve is to learn from the mistakes you make on practice tests, which is why we begin our discussion with Kaplan's Why I Missed It Sheets (WIMIS). The Post-Phrasing strategy discussed in the following section builds on the WIMIS, helping you go the extra mile to begin thinking more like the makers of the MCAT. Subsequently, we'll talk about a simple approach for managing your pacing on Test Day, and then we'll discuss what you can do to build your test-taking stamina. We'll close with a discussion of one final advantage you can give yourself for CARS: a stronger vocabulary.

12.1 Learning from Your Mistakes

At this juncture you have read quite a bit about how to approach CARS, have had the opportunity to practice, and should have completed at least one Full-Length Exam. Now it is time to reflect on your performance and adjust your study plan based on your personal test-taking pathologies, identifiable patterns in your past errors that can help to guide your future CARS studying.

Bridge

Need some help identifying the question type for your Why I Missed It Sheets? Don't forget to review Chapters 9, 10, and 11 of *MCAT CARS Review* for thorough coverage of each question type.

WHY I MISSED IT SHEETS

It can be overwhelming to try to discern what your strengths and areas of opportunity are by looking at an entire CARS section all at once. Rather, take time to analyze each question you answered incorrectly. One way to help manage this process—and to keep a clear record of your performance over time—is to set up **Why I Missed It Sheets (WIMIS)**. Create a document with four columns: question number, question type, topic (or discipline), and "Why I Missed It." In the first column, make a list compiling all of the items you answered incorrectly on the test. In the second column, identify the question type based on the Kaplan classifications we reviewed in the previous three chapters. The third column should include the topic, or academic discipline, for the passage. Lastly, in column four, take time to review your incorrect response and identify the specific reason why you got the question wrong and missed those points. Table 12.1 demonstrates what a WIMIS should look like.

Question Number	Question Type	Topic/ Discipline	Why I Missed It
Full-Length *X*, #12	Detail	Music	Misinterpreted the question stem, leading me to the wrong paragraph for information.
Full-Length *X*, #21	Strengthen–Weaken (Within)	Art	Chose a piece of evidence that would strengthen the critics' point of view, but was looking to strengthen the author's point of view.
Full-Length *X*, #38	Inference	Population Health	Chose an answer choice that *may* be true based on the information in the passage but does not have to be— Inference questions have answers that *must* be true based on the passage.
Full-Length *X*, #54	Main Idea	Psychology	Answer choice was too narrow, only describing two of the paragraphs but not the entire passage.

Table 12.1. Sample Why I Missed It Sheet (WIMIS)

The most important element of this table is the *Why I Missed It* column. Do not just categorize this with a generic *I didn't understand* or *careless mistake*. Such comments will not help you understand why you missed the question. Instead, choose something that is—contradictory as this may sound—as specific and as generalizable as possible. Did you read the question wrong? Did you miss a major point in the passage? Were you unable to see the relevance of a piece of information in the passage or how new information pertained to the passage? Write things that identify the flaw in the thinking process as specifically as possible, while also making sure that you can extrapolate what you learn from that question to future questions. Consider the following pairs of "bad" and "good" examples:

Bad: *I missed this because the answer choice declares that* Beowulf *was written by an aristocrat, but the passage said that the author was only "probably" a member of the royal court.*

Good: *I missed this because the answer choice stated something as fact that the passage's author did not.*

Bad: *I missed this because I thought the question was asking for the author's opinion on Mendelssohn's work, but it was actually asking for his opinion on the critics of Mendelssohn's work.*

Good: *I missed this because I confused which opinion a question stem was asking for.*

Bad: *I missed this because I recognized "unmoved mover" from the question stem, which is in paragraph 3, but the answer they were looking for actually comes from the description of the "Central Headquarters" sentence in paragraph 4.*

Good: *I missed this because I failed to see how the paragraphs fit together (how an idea in one paragraph is further explained in subsequent paragraphs) before moving on to the questions.*

When reviewing your WIMIS, compare the question type column to the topic/discipline column to narrow the scope of your future study plan. Is there a recognizable pattern you can utilize to optimize your performance? For instance, are you repeatedly missing *Reasoning Within the Text* question types? Or are you only missing this category of question types in Philosophical passages? Use the WIMIS to plan which passage varieties you'll focus on in the future or to determine which chapters you need to reread in *MCAT CARS Review*. You want to make sure that you are moving forward with a plan that specifically supports your areas of opportunity.

If you repeatedly read questions incorrectly, you are not alone—it is extremely common for students to misread or misinterpret questions in CARS, which can lead to selecting an incorrect answer. Making an oversight and missing a word in a question or reading too rapidly and not fully understanding what is being asked can lead to errors. Take your time to read the questions critically to ensure you understand what is being asked. Remember, establishing the question type and finding clues in the question stem about where to research are critical components of the Plan step of the Kaplan Method for CARS Questions. As you review your practice tests, reexamine the questions and the answers you selected that were incorrect. In hindsight, when looking at the question a second time, do you find yourself shaking your head because you simply misinterpreted what was being asked? This could indicate that you are reading the question stems too hastily and moving on to the process of answering the question before you even know what you're supposed to be answering! If this is the case, force yourself to take the extra time to reword a difficult question stem, so it becomes clear to you precisely what it is asking. This is not wasted

Real World

In medical school, you'll attend morbidity and mortality (M&M) conferences, in which physicians review clinical and medical errors, patient complications, and other healthcare quality measures to investigate the root causes of problems in order to fix them directly. This is not dissimilar to creating Why I Missed It Sheets—you can only improve if you know what you're doing wrong!

time—having more clarity on the question *behind the question* (that is, what the question is *really* asking) will allow you to create a Plan more quickly, Execute that Plan more efficiently, and Answer the question more accurately in less time.

If your WIMIS demonstrates a pattern in which you keep missing the same question types, then start to triage those questions. First, go back and reread the appropriate chapter in *MCAT CARS Review* so you can begin to recognize these question types with greater ease. Chapters 9, 10, and 11 introduced the eight major question types and highlighted the common question stems that fall into each type. Remember that each question type has an associated strategy that will help you accomplish the task or tasks required by the question stem.

Finally, take note of the Wrong Answer Pathologies of the incorrect answers you chose. Simply knowing the Wrong Answer Pathologies that most often sway you from choosing the correct answer is enough to help you avoid falling for the same traps in future tests. For example, if you know that you frequently choose Out of Scope answer choices in Main Idea questions, then ask yourself *Is this answer truly within the confines of the passage, or does it bring in something else?* before finalizing your answer for Main Idea questions in the future.

12.2 Thinking Like the Testmaker: Post-Phrasing

With **post-phrasing,** you go over both why incorrect answers are wrong and why correct answers are right. This strategy is especially helpful if you frequently experience the classic test-taking dilemma: *I can usually narrow it down to two answer choices, and then I always go for the wrong one!*

Post-phrasing begins with your WIMIS. Once you have completed your WIMIS, identify which questions you answered incorrectly and make a note of the correct answer. The post-phrasing process then requires you to articulate in your own words what the question stem says. You may find it helpful to write down your reworded question on a piece of scratch paper or in a word processor. Your focus in this first step should be decoding what the question stem is actually asking you to do. Determine the question type and write or state out loud what the appropriate Plan step is for such a question.

Once you've determined the appropriate Plan for the question, Execute the plan, writing out your prediction for the correct response. It's essential to take the time to write this down: many students find that a nebulous or poorly focused prediction is what keeps them from being able to Answer the question at the end of the Kaplan Method for CARS Questions. The more you practice writing out your predictions during the post-phrasing process, the more routine making predictions will become.

Bridge

Knowing your personal test-taking pathologies is essential to improving your score. In addition to looking at the question types, topics or disciplines, and how you read question stems, don't forget to look at Kaplan's classifications of Wrong Answer Pathologies (Faulty Use of Detail, Out of Scope, Opposite, and Distortion), discussed in Chapter 8 of *MCAT CARS Review*.

You may notice that the description of post-phrasing, thus far, basically describes a regimented and very deliberate use of the Kaplan Method for CARS Questions. But at the end, the focus will not be on matching your prediction anymore; after all, you already know the correct answer because you're reviewing a question you answered incorrectly. Instead, turn your attention to the incorrect answers. Determine why each incorrect answer is unsuitable. Does it fail to match your prediction? Does it have a common Wrong Answer Pathology? Are there other subtle flaws in logic or reasoning that misrepresent the author's arguments? By taking the time to write out an explanation for each of the incorrect answers, you'll begin to see the correlation between questions and correct answers, as well as reasons for eliminating wrong answers in future questions that you encounter.

Alternatively, post-phrasing can be used as an exercise to improve your recognition of Wrong Answer Pathologies in passages you haven't seen yet. Consider practicing with a few passages following the steps below:

1. Find a fresh CARS passage from your Kaplan online resources, as well as its explanations.

2. Go through and circle all the correct answers for the passage. Don't read the explanations, just circle and set the answers aside for now.

3. Outline the passage as you normally would.

4. When you work on the questions, do so in a fundamentally different way: as above, the goal here is not to find the right answers (as you have already identified them) but to reason why each incorrect answer is wrong. Read the right answer to be sure you understand it, but spend more time identifying the types of wrong answers presented by the other choices.

5. Look at the explanations for each incorrect answer choice and compare them with your notes. If there are any major omissions or other discrepancies in your explanations, be sure to note them prominently. The more you practice, though, the closer you should find the correspondence between your post-phrasing notes and Kaplan's explanations.

It won't take long before you find yourself recognizing the correct answer and thinking *this one just feels right*. Having spent time concentrating on identifying wrong answers, you will begin to see the patterns emerge and the subtle flaws in these choices make themselves more pronounced. Taking the time to post-phrase will expand your awareness of how the test is written and what the expectations are for CARS questions. Furthermore, you will refine your thought process, and your approach to passages and questions, making you better prepared for Test Day.

Bridge

In addition to Wrong Answer Pathologies, take time to review the Signs of a Healthy Answer presented in Chapter 8 of *MCAT CARS Review*. These include appropriate scope, agreement with the author, and "hedging" language that creates weaker claims.

12.3 Improving Your Timing

Proper management of the clock can make a significant difference to your score in any section, but the timing constraints in the CARS section differ from those of the other sections. Consider a few basic facts about the CARS section:

- It lasts 90 minutes.
- There are 53 questions.

Because all of the points actually come from answering the questions, you'll want to ensure that you allot them enough time. Passages vary in difficulty, meaning that some will certainly take longer to read than others, but as a rule of thumb you should aim to complete reading and Outlining the passage in about 4 minutes. This leaves you with an average of 50–60 seconds per question. Keep in mind that the number of questions associated with a passage can vary from 5 to 7, meaning that a more precise expectation for completing a passage and its questions is somewhere between 8 and 10 minutes.

PACING GUIDELINES

Now, trying to ensure that each passage only takes 4 minutes and each question only 50–60 seconds would actually be counterproductive: not only would you lose a substantial amount of time checking the clock, you'd likely heighten your anxiety whenever you came across the inevitable question that takes a little extra time to get through. A better approach to managing your time is to check your timing only at a limited number of predetermined points during the section. We recommend checking the clock after every other passage. Assuming that you take 9 minutes to read a passage and answer its questions, you should ideally be no more than 18 minutes further into the section each time you check the clock.

MCAT Expertise

While it is most common to have five to seven questions associated with a given passage, there have been instances of passages with only four or as many as eight questions. This should not significantly impact how you approach these passages, although— all else being equal—a passage with eight questions will give you more points for the same amount of reading.

While this approach does not leave you much of a cushion for going back to previous passages and questions, this is by far the easiest way to master pacing. Given that each passage contains between 500 and 600 words, jumping between passages is a far less viable option in CARS than in any of the science sections, where passages can be less than half that length. While it's recommended that you skip passages that you decide in your Scan step will take you too long, we do not recommend giving up in the middle of a passage you decided to work on to return to later. Once you decide to work on a passage, commit to finishing it.

MANAGING QUESTION TIMING

While these guidelines are useful for managing the section, it can still be tricky to master how to split your time between reading the passages and answering the questions. In your online resources, we record the time spent working on each question so you can get a sense of which questions take you longer than others. (Note that this mechanism requires you to click on the question when you begin working on it to accurately record this information.) Keep in mind that the first question of each passage will build in the time you spend critically reading and Outlining the passage in the beginning. Thus, you should strive to have the first question of each set answered in fewer than 5 minutes, and every subsequent question should be close to the 50- to 60-second mark calculated above.

Once you have a better sense of what types of passages and questions take you longer to complete, you should use this information in conjunction with what you've learned from each WIMIS to guide your *now* or *later* decisions in the first step of each method (Scan for passages and Assess for questions). Doing the passages that are easier for you first will allow you to get ahead on the timing curve. Similarly, saving the toughest questions for the end of each set will allow you to gain additional familiarity with the passage as you work on its more manageable questions. Because questions can repeat the same theme, you may even find the answer to a challenging question while working on an easier question later in the set.

MCAT Expertise

If the seconds ticking down cause you too much anxiety, an alternative way of working on your timing is to use the timer on your phone or some other timepiece to "time up"—that is, to count upwards from zero to see how much time it's taking you to read the passage and for each question. Timers with "lap" functions can be especially useful because these can record how long each question takes. Generally, this method works best with only one or two passages at a time.

12.4 Building Endurance

Preparing for the MCAT is like preparing for a marathon. You cannot run 1 or 2 miles a day for two months and then expect to be successful in a 26.2-mile marathon. Runners vary their running time and build up to the 26.2 miles, routinely running long distances in preparation for marathon day.

How often are you studying and for how long? If you are only studying in 30- or 60-minute increments, it could be that when you sit down to complete a Full-Length Exam that you have not built up your endurance for that type of scenario. Not only do you need to study and practice regularly, but you also need to simulate the Test Day experience of concentrating for 6 hours and 15 minutes of testing time. Gear up for practice tests—and Test Day itself—by periodically holding long study and practice sessions. When working on CARS, try studying in 90-minute increments to mimic the amount of time you'll have for this section.

12.5 Enhancing Your Vocabulary

The AAMC claims that there's no outside content required for the CARS Section of the MCAT, but in truth this is not 100 percent accurate. If you're a student whose first language isn't English, you know this all too well. Even though very few questions hinge on knowing the definition of a piece of jargon from outside knowledge, it is nevertheless a tremendous asset to go into Test Day with a strong vocabulary. If nothing else, you can benefit by becoming more comfortable with academic writing in the various disciplines that the AAMC includes in the CARS section by familiarizing yourself with plenty of examples.

The Kaplan and AAMC Full-Length Exams are of course the best place to go to get samples of CARS-style passages and questions. But students who want to go the extra mile also have the option of practicing with outside reading.

READING PLAN

The more often you read, the stronger your reading comprehension skills become, and the faster you evolve into a more efficient reader. This is because you build up a wider array of words you recognize by sight and thus require less time to decipher a text. To prepare for CARS, read on a consistent basis; this will increase your reading speed so that you can maneuver swiftly through passages.

Set up a regimented reading schedule for at least 18 minutes a day, which is just enough time to get through two passages according to the guidelines given above.

Bridge

While you will not be expected to know the definition of a piece of jargon from outside knowledge, Definition-in-Context questions hinge on your ability to determine the meaning of a word or phrase from the rest of the passage. These questions are discussed in Chapter 9 of *MCAT CARS Review*.

Or, keep an array of reading materials handy for when you have time available. This could consist of a list of links kept on a smart phone or other wireless-enabled device. It is surprising how much time we spend waiting—for a friend at a coffee shop, for a group to go out in the evening, for a professor to arrive to class, in a hallway or lounge before a meeting—that could be used productively, sharpening reading skills to prepare for CARS.

When selecting materials, try to simulate the variety of passages you'll encounter on Test Day, with a blend of texts from both the humanities and the social sciences. Use your WIMIS to determine which types of passages cause you the greatest confusion or frustration, the ones that slow you down the most on your Full-Length exams. Focus on reading those types of passages in particular; the more you read these difficult texts, the more familiar you will become with their jargon and other conventions, and the less intimidating these passages will start to seem. Consider using one of the following online services to find academic journal articles in the disciplines that give you the most trouble:

- JSTOR (jstor.org)
- Oxford Journals (oxfordjournals.org)
- Google Scholar (scholar.google.com)
- Project MUSE (muse.jhu.edu)
- The Directory of Open Access Journals (doaj.org)
- Sage Journals (online.sagepub.com)

Whenever you come across a word that you don't recognize, stop and take a moment to look that word up, and write down its definition *in your own words*. Keeping a list of these new terms and looking over them periodically will go a long way toward building your vocabulary. As your vocabulary expands, you will be able to recognize words or infer their meaning more swiftly, which will increase your efficiency both with reading and Outlining the passage and with tackling question stems and answer choices.

In addition to learning the meanings of new words, it's also helpful to become acquainted with the major themes and concepts that are distinctive to each of the humanities and social sciences that appear on the CARS section. Familiarity with a concept can allow you to glean more from a passage when it's mentioned, enabling you to read more quickly if the text simply repeats what you've already learned. Be careful, however, not to bring in any ideas that the passage does not include when answering its questions (there's a reason Out of Scope is a common Wrong Answer Pathology)! Because there are only a limited number of passages in CARS, the likelihood that you have read about the exact same scenario presented in a CARS passage is not high, but it is very likely that you will have read about similar topics.

Additionally, any form of academic reading forces you to think critically about the ideas the author is presenting. Just as when you practice with passages in CARS, try Outlining a few paragraphs of an academic article. Focus on how the author structures the argument: What conclusion does he or she want the audience to reach? What evidence is used to support that conclusion? Are there any flaws in the author's logic? Focused, regular reading will help prepare you for CARS by bolstering your reading comprehension and reasoning skills, as well as your comfort with academic texts and the challenges they bring.

Conclusion

Medical schools want to admit students with strong reasoning skills because higher-order thinking is necessary for both appropriately diagnosing patients and conducting groundbreaking research. When given a list of symptoms and concerns, a physician needs to generate a differential diagnosis—a list of the potential ailments described by the symptoms. From this list, the medical team must rule out unlikely diagnoses and provide evidence for the most likely diagnosis. What starts out as a list of a hundred possible causes of headache—from migraines and tension-type headaches to intracranial bleeds and brain tumors—is reduced to one most likely cause after asking appropriate questions (*When did the headache start? Where do you feel the headache? Have you ever had anything similar before?*), performing a thorough physical exam (cranial nerve function, eye exam, looking for evidence of trauma), and running appropriate laboratory and imaging tests (head CT, MRI, inflammatory markers).

Patients want to trust in the expertise of their doctors, and you want to ensure that you are able to deliver the best treatment to your patients. The same skills in CARS that enable you to determine the author's perspective, distinguish his or her voice from that of the support offered by others, predict a response to a question, and match your predictions (while eliminating incorrect answers) will serve you well as a physician. In the future, you may not be expected to think critically about dance theory, musicology, archaeology, and linguistics, but you will have to synthesize disparate pieces of information, consider assumptions about patient care, and respond appropriately to all parts of your patients' questions—both what they say and what they leave for you to infer. As pointed out in this chapter, the skills tested in the *Critical Analysis and Reasoning Skills* section can always be improved through pointed and actionable review of your past performance. Congratulations on reaching the end of *MCAT Critical Analysis and Reasoning Skills Review.* Though this book now comes to an end, for you this is merely a beginning—good luck on the MCAT, and in all your endeavors in medicine!

CONCEPT AND STRATEGY SUMMARY

Learning from Your Mistakes

- Create Why I Missed It Sheets (WIMIS) to look for your test-taking pathology patterns.

  - Make a four-column table: question number, question type, topic/discipline, and "Why I Missed It."

  - In the Why I Missed It column, describe the error you made in the question as specifically as possible (with respect to the thought pattern), but in a way that allows you to extrapolate what you learn from that question to future questions.

  - Look for patterns in your WIMIS.

- If you misread questions, be sure to slow down and reword the question stem to make sure you know what question you are actually trying to answer.

- Reread the relevant chapters in *MCAT Critical Analysis and Reasoning Skills Review* as needed.

Thinking Like the Testmaker: Post-Phrasing

- Find a CARS passage from your Kaplan online resources, as well as its explanations. This could be a passage you have already read or a new one.

- Go through and circle all the correct answers for the passage. Don't read the explanations—just circle and set the answers aside for now.

- Outline the passage as you normally would.

- When you work on the questions, do so in a fundamentally different way: the goal here is not to find the right answers (as you have already identified them) but to reason why each incorrect answer is wrong. Read the right answer to be sure you understand it, but spend more time identifying the types of wrong answers presented by the other choices.

- Look at the explanations for each incorrect answer choice and compare them with your notes. If there are any major omissions or other discrepancies in your explanations, be sure to note them prominently.

Improving Your Timing

- Aim to read a passage in about 4 minutes; aim to answer each question in about 50–60 seconds.

- Each passage and its questions together should take somewhere between 8 and 10 minutes.

Building Endurance

- Increase stamina by studying in 90-minute increments when possible (equal to the amount of time for the CARS section).

- Periodically, simulate the Test Day experience with study and practice for 6 hours and 15 minutes (equal to the amount of testing time).

Enhancing Your Vocabulary

- Read academic texts for at least 18 minutes a day to sharpen reading skills in preparation for CARS.

- Choose articles on topics that cause you trouble on Full-Length Exams (as revealed by your WIMIS).

- Practice Outlining using these articles.

Notes

Notes

Notes

Notes

Notes

Notes

Notes

Notes

Notes

Notes

Notes

Notes